Abracadabra VIOLIN

THIRD EDITION

The way to learn through songs and tunes

Peter Davey

A&C BLACK · LONDON

Contents

step 1
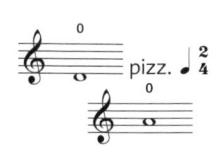
1. Pizz on D
2. Pizz A pizza!
3. Bobby Shafto

step 2
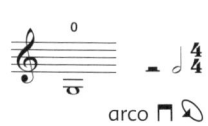
4. When the saints go marching in
5. Supercalifragilistic-expialidocious
6. A tisket, a tasket
7. Little playmates
8. Mobile phone
9. Fiddle fanfare (duet/trio)

step 3

10. A friend in DEED
11. One finger dance (duet)
12. Eee-abba-dabba-dee!
13. Spinning wheel
14. A stitch in time

step 4

15. Frère Jacques
16. Welsh lullaby (duet)
17. Windmill song (duet)
18. Hot cross buns (duet)
19. Merrily we roll along

step 5

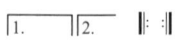

20. Pease pudding hot
21. Clown dance
22. Road monsters
23. Au clair de la lune
24. Twinkle, twinkle little bow
25. Miss Mary Mac
26. The song that never stops (duet)
27. Whistle while you work (duet)

step 6

28. Secret agents (duet)
29. Little bird
30. Summer shine (duet)
31. Halfway down the stairs
32. Old MacDonald
    G major scale

step 7
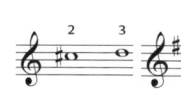
33. Brown bread (duet)
34. Big Ben (duet)
35. Turn the glasses over (round)
36. Off to France in the morning
    D major scale

step 8

37. Racing driver (round)
38. Long, long ago (duet)
39. Ode to joy (duet)
40. The way you look tonight
41. (Meet the) Flintstones

step 9

42. I came from Alabama
43. Morningtown ride
44. Troika
45. Daydreamer

step 10

46. Roses from the South
47. Lavender's blue (duet)
48. Call of the carousel

step 11

49. We all stand together (duet)
50. Edelweiss
51. On top of Old Smokey (duet)
52. London's burning (round)
53. The hippopotamus song

step 12

♩. f.b. 54 London Bridge (duet)
55 Tea for two
56 Stand by me

step 13

57 Skye boat song (duet)
58 Jupiter
59 Feed the birds

step 14

♩ ♩ cresc. 60 Kalinka
61 The old bazaar in Cairo
mp mf 62 Muck! (round)
63 Waltz
64 Puff the magic dragon (duet)
♫ ♪ 65 Dumplins

step 15

6/8 66 Row, row, row your boat (round)
67 Pop! goes the weasel
68 Dance of the cuckoos (duet)
69 The shepherdess (round)
  D major arpeggio
  G major arpeggio
70 We're off to see the Wizard

step 16

 71 Egyptian snake dance
72 Shalom (round)
73 Summer is icumen in (round)
74 Part of your world (duet)

step 17

♪ 75 Short'nin' bread (duet)
76 What shall we do with the drunken sailor? (duet)
♫ 77 Winter wonderland
78 EastEnders

step 18

⌒ 79 Happy birthday (duet)
80 Heigh-ho
81 The Addams family (duet)
82 The mocking bird
83 Chim chim cher-ee

step 19

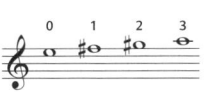 84 Ragamuffin's rag
  A major scale
  A major arpeggio
 85 Who will buy?
  G major scale (two octaves)
  G major arpeggio (two octaves)
86 Beauty and the Beast (duet)

step 20

 rall. 87 Barcarolle (duet)
88 Nocturne

Acknowledgements
Index
Glossary

step 1

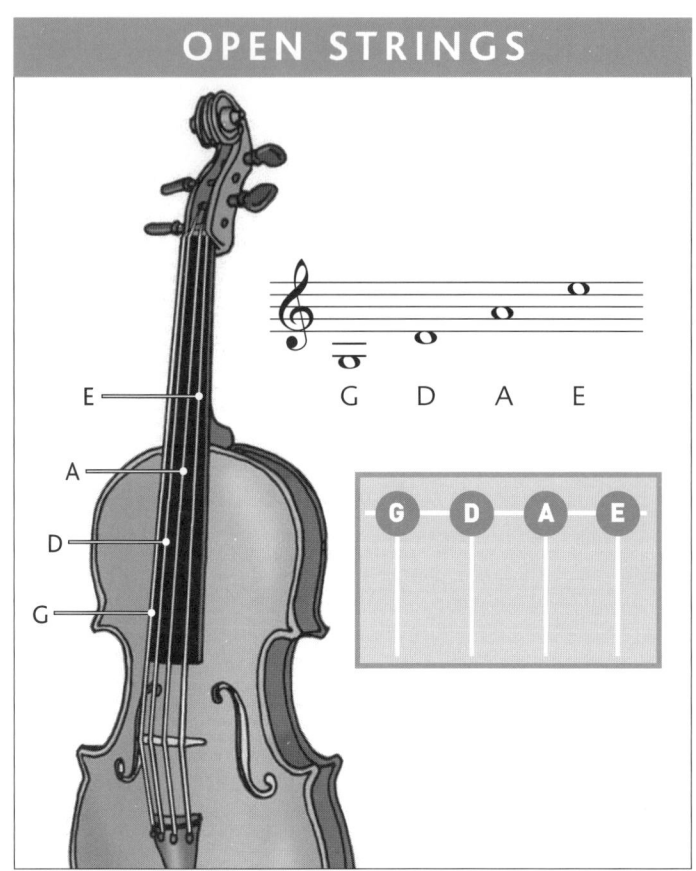

OPEN STRINGS

 Pluck your violin strings to play the tunes in step 1. This technique is called **pizzicato**, or **pizz**.

♩ crotchet – worth one beat.

2/4 time signature – this means there are two crotchet beats to the bar.

Play your part in *Pizz on D* twice.

1 Pizz on D (2-3)

CH/VSP

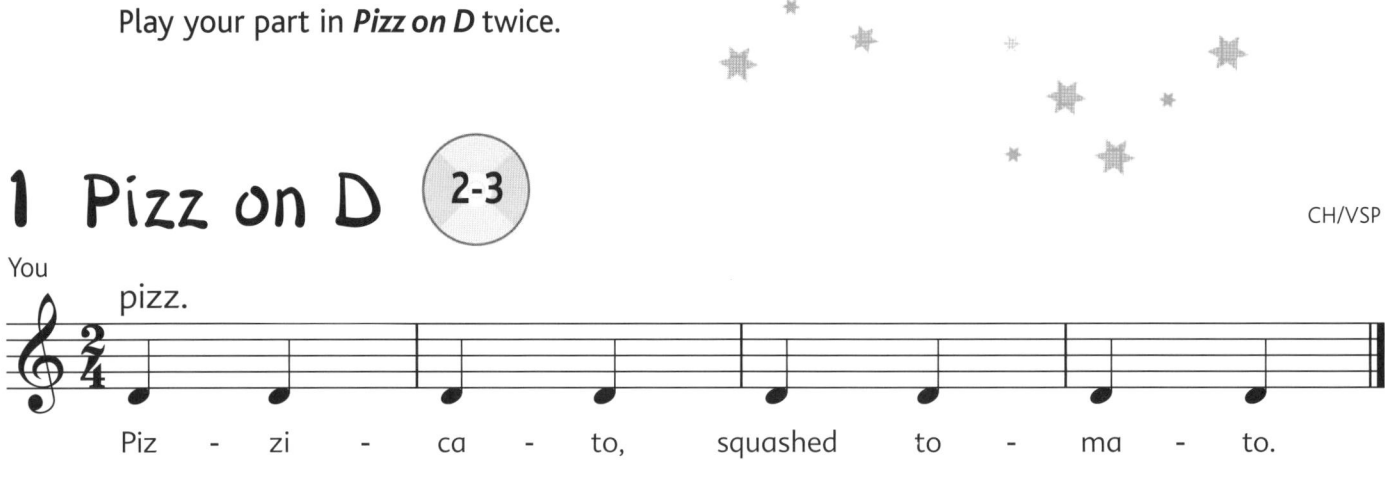

You
pizz.
Piz - zi - ca - to, squashed to - ma - to.

Your teacher
pizz.
Piz - zi - ca - to D string, lis - ten to the sound ring.

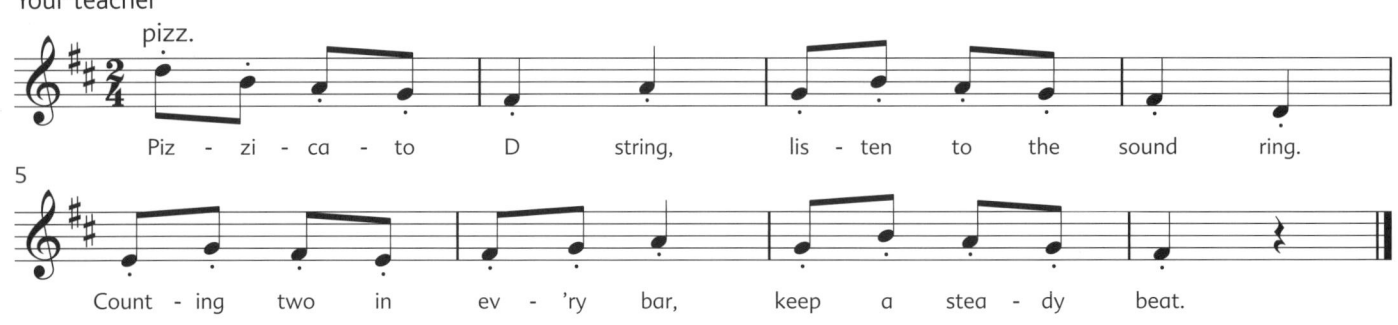

Count - ing two in ev - 'ry bar, keep a stea - dy beat.

Play your part in *Pizz A pizza!* twice.

To make a longer piece, play *Pizz on D*, *Pizz A pizza!* and *Pizz on D* again, without pausing between the tunes.

2 Pizz A pizza!

CH/JS

3 Bobby Shafto

traditional

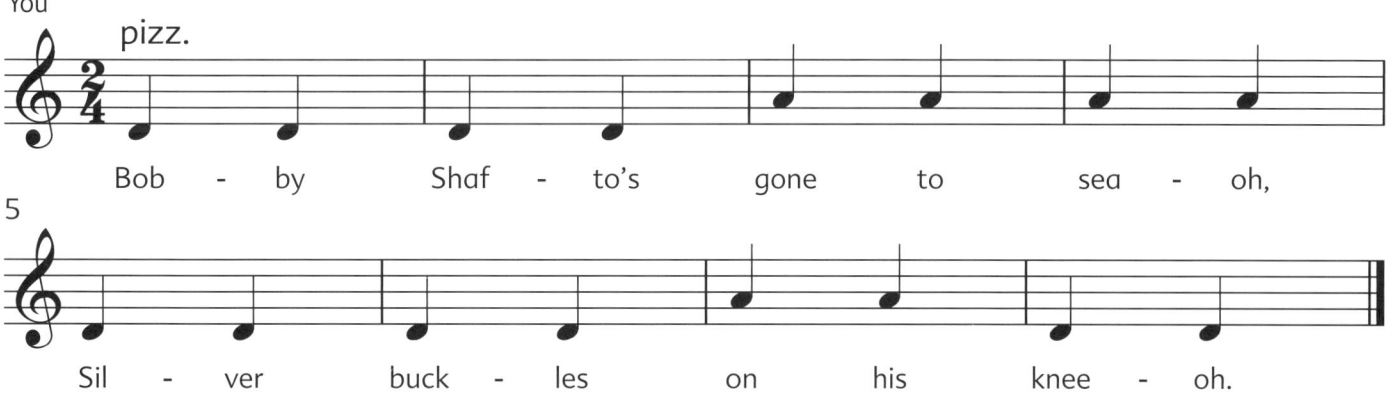

 Play each of the tunes in step 1 twice through with your teacher.

1st time: you sing or say the words to your tune;
2nd time: ask your teacher to sing the words to their part.

step 2

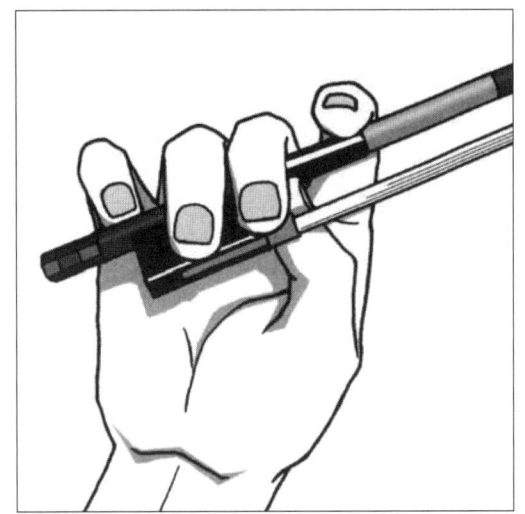

DOWN-BOW

From heel to point

⭐ $\frac{4}{4}$ **time signature** – four crotchet beats to the bar.

𝅗𝅥 **minim** – worth two crotchet beats.

▬ **minim rest** – it lasts for two crotchet beats of silence.

From now on, play all the tunes **arco** – with your bow – unless pizzicato is indicated.

⊓ marks a **down-bow**.

 tells you to lift your bow in a circular motion to prepare for the next down-bow.

4 When the saints go marching in   8-9
(pupil's part)

traditional spiritual

 ⁍ **crotchet rest** – it lasts for one beat of silence.

5 Supercalifragilisticexpialidocious 10-11

Richard M Sherman and Robert B Sherman

4 When the saints go marching in

(teacher's part)

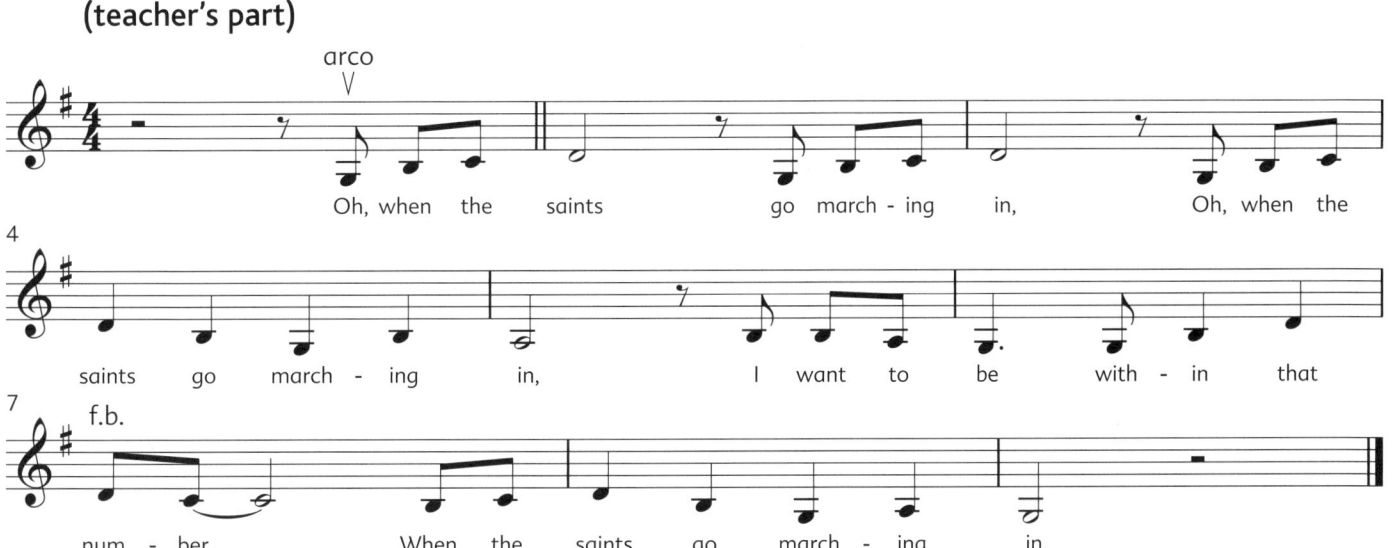

6 A-tisket, a-tasket 12-13

words CH, music traditional

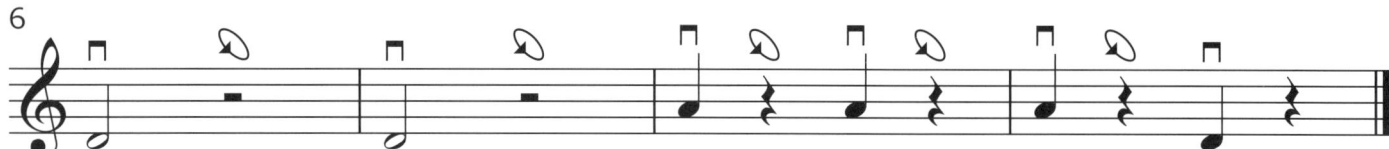
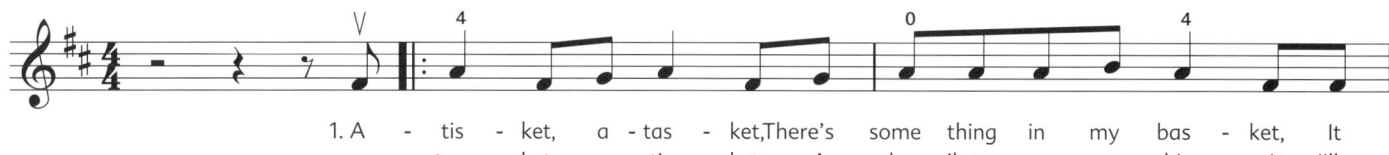

1. A-tisket, a-tasket, There's something in my basket, It smells so sweet, it's good to eat, I'd bet you'd like to taste it. 2. A
2. tasket, a-tisket, A choc-'late orange biscuit, I'll eat it now before you can, 'Cos I don't want to waste it!

V marks an **up-bow**.

The bowing ⊓ V ⊓ tells you to play a **down-bow**, an **up-bow** and a **down-bow**, without lifting your bow off the string in between.

DOWN-BOW — From heel to point

UP-BOW — From point to heel

7 Little playmates 14-15

F X Chwatal

step 3

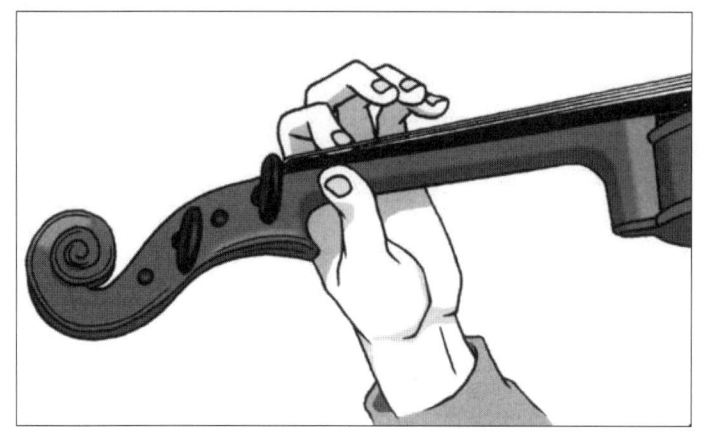
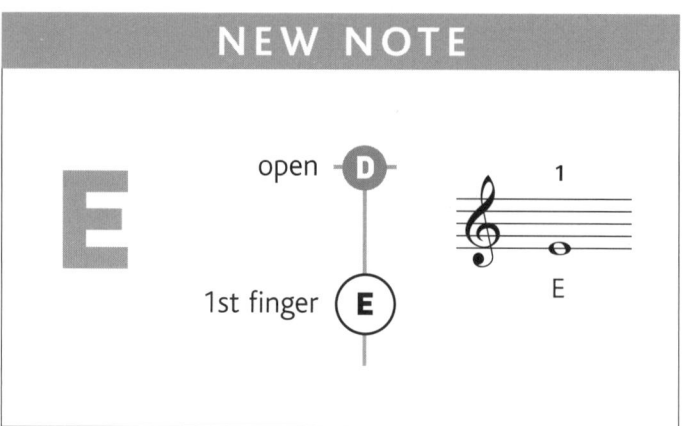

⭐ Play and sing this song with a friend.
It is like a conversation, in which you and your friend play question and answer phrases.

10 A friend in DEED

CH/JS

You
D E E D, You're a friend in - deed.

Your friend
Al - ways there to help when I'm in need.

Both
So we're friends to - ge - ther, yes in - deed.

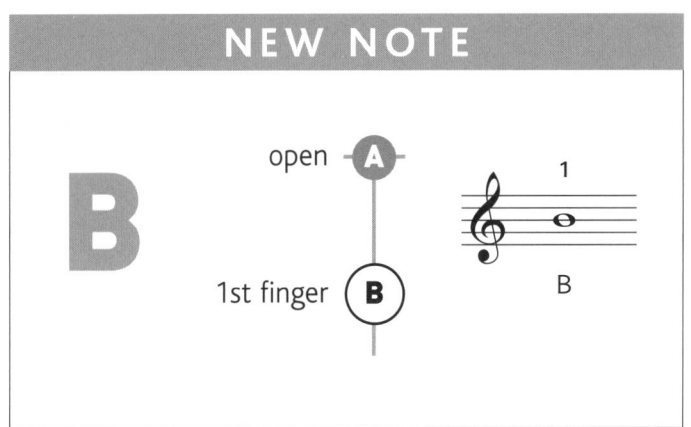

NEW NOTE

:|| **repeat mark** – tells you to go back to the beginning and repeat the music.

In the second part of *One finger dance* the open strings D and A are played together – this is called **double stopping**.

11 One finger dance (duet)

PD

You

Your friend

12 Eee-abba-dabba-dee!

CH

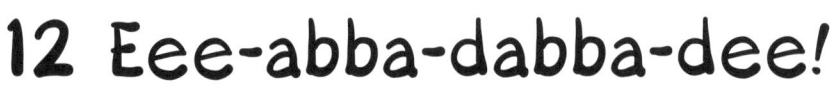

E   A   B   B   A,   D   A   B   B   A,

D   E   E,   Fred and me,   Eee - ab - ba - dab - ba - dee!

13 Spinning wheel

PD

Push tread - le, drive spin - dle, Round goes the spin - ning wheel.

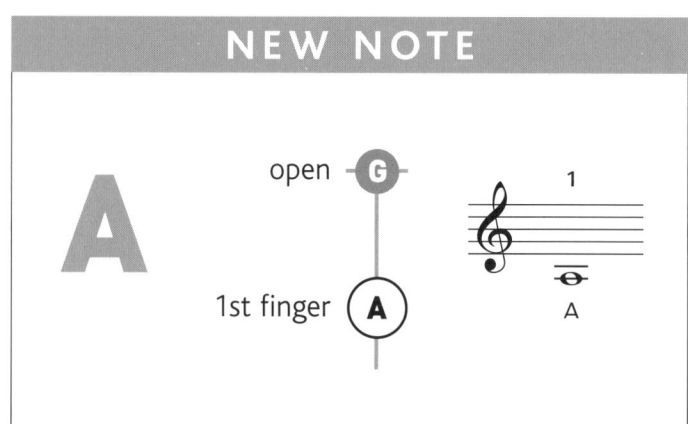

NEW NOTE

A — open G / 1st finger A

14 A stitch in time

CH

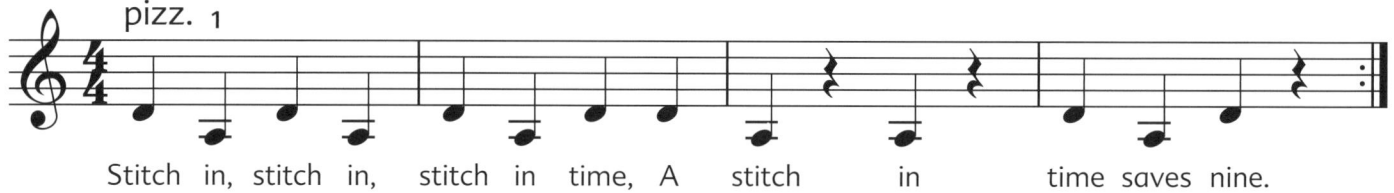

pizz.

Stitch in, stitch in, stitch in time, A stitch in time saves nine.

 Try playing **A stitch in time** while your teacher plays **Spinning wheel**. Then swap over.

step 4

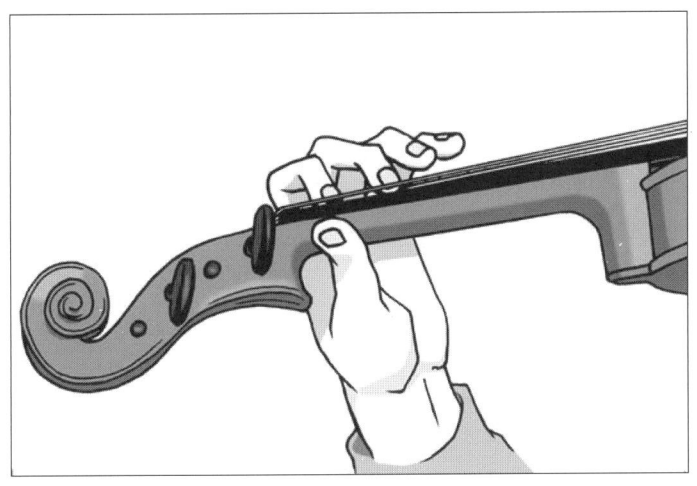
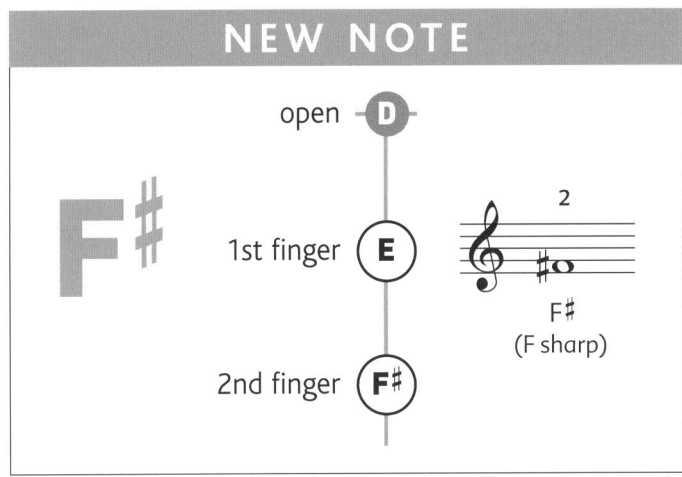

 # is called a **sharp**. F# sounds a little higher than F.

In *Frère Jacques* you play a repeated one-bar phrase. A phrase repeated like this is called an **ostinato**.

15 Frère Jacques

traditional French

Ostinato 1

 Play **Ostinato 2** eight times, while your teacher plays the tune. Then try the same with **Ostinato 3**.

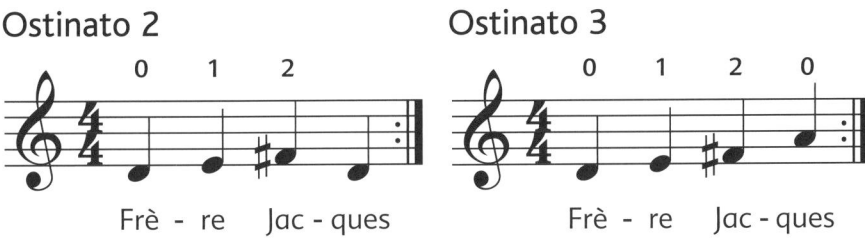

Play *Welsh lullaby* like this:

arco – for a baby dolphin

pizzicato – for a baby kangaroo

with your eyes shut – for a baby dormouse

16 Welsh lullaby (duet)

traditional Welsh

 ♯ The sharp sign affects all the notes of the same pitch in the rest of the bar. For example, the fourth note in bar 1 of *Windmill song* is F♯ not F.

17 Windmill song (duet)

words CH, music PD

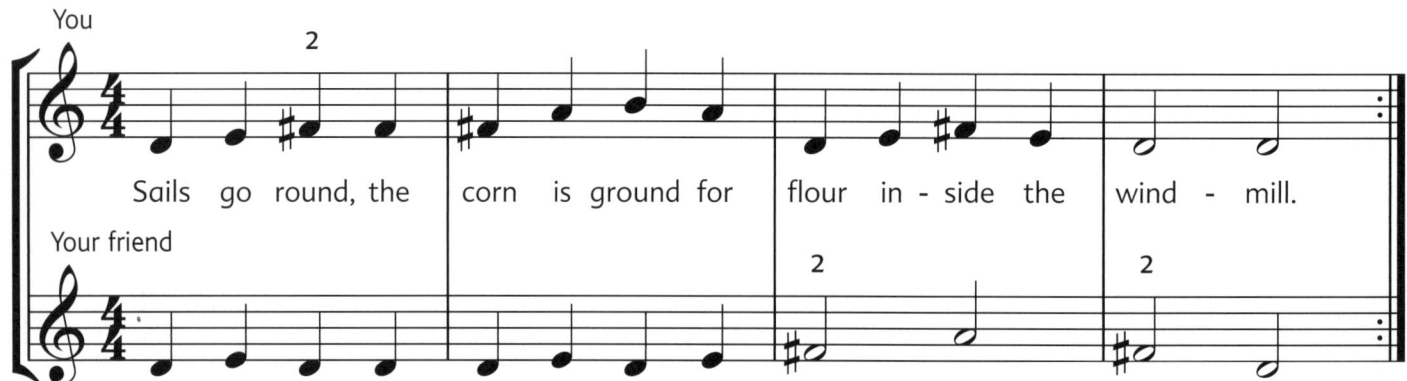

 ♪ **quaver** – worth half a crotchet beat.

Two quavers may be written like this: ♫

The next two pieces begin on F♯, played with the 2nd finger. Make sure the F♯ is in tune before you start the piece. Climb up to it by playing D (open), then E (1st finger), then F♯ (2nd finger).

18 Hot cross buns (duet)

traditional

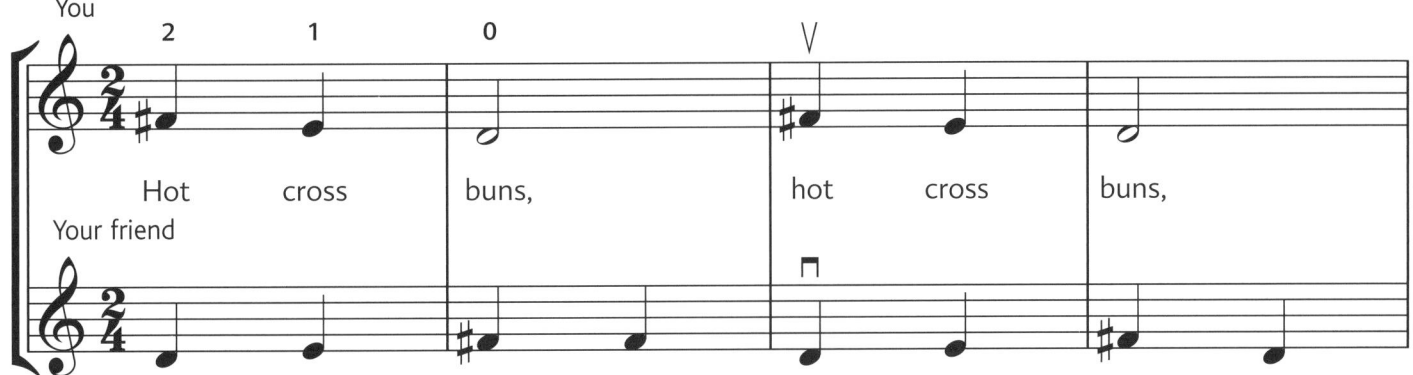

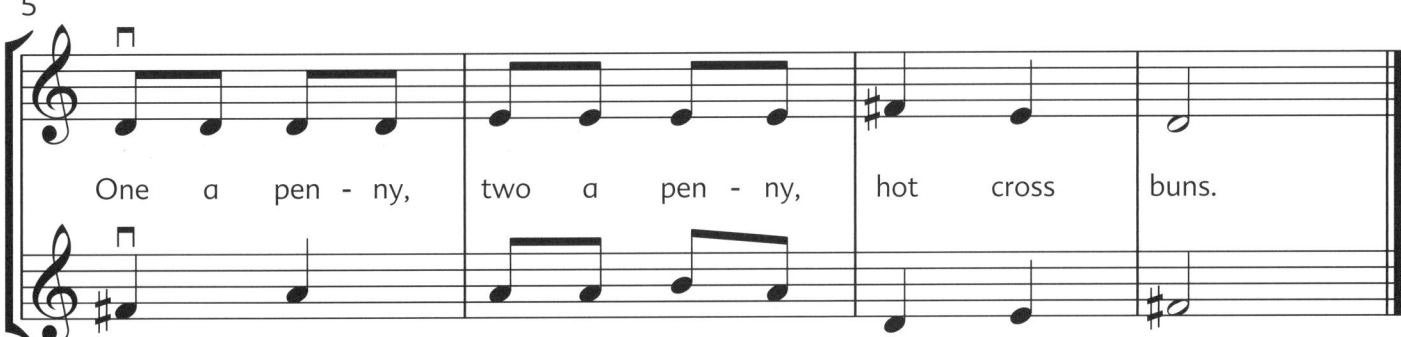

 Look at the last bar in no. 19. Do you remember the name of this technique? (Look at no. 11.)

19 Merrily we roll along 40-41

traditional

Swung

step 5

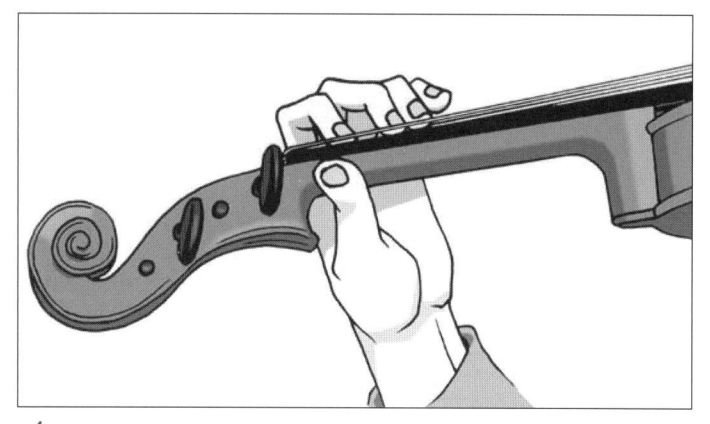

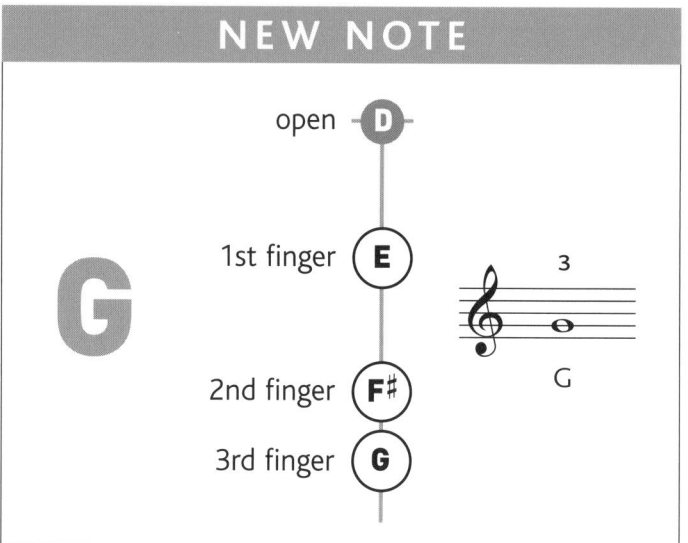

NEW NOTE

G — open D, 1st finger E, 2nd finger F#, 3rd finger G

15/5

20 Pease pudding hot 42-43

traditional

Pease pud - ding hot, pease pud - ding cold.
Pease pud - ding in the pot grow - ing mould!

★ Ask your friend to play the ostinato accompaniment opposite.

15/5

21 Clown dance 44-45

traditional French

1.
2.

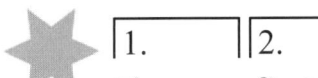

These are **first time** and **second time bars**. When you repeat the music, miss out the first time bar and go straight to the second time bar.

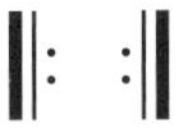

 When there are two repeat marks, repeat the passage of music between them.

22 Road monsters

46-47

words CH/SR, music traditional Israeli

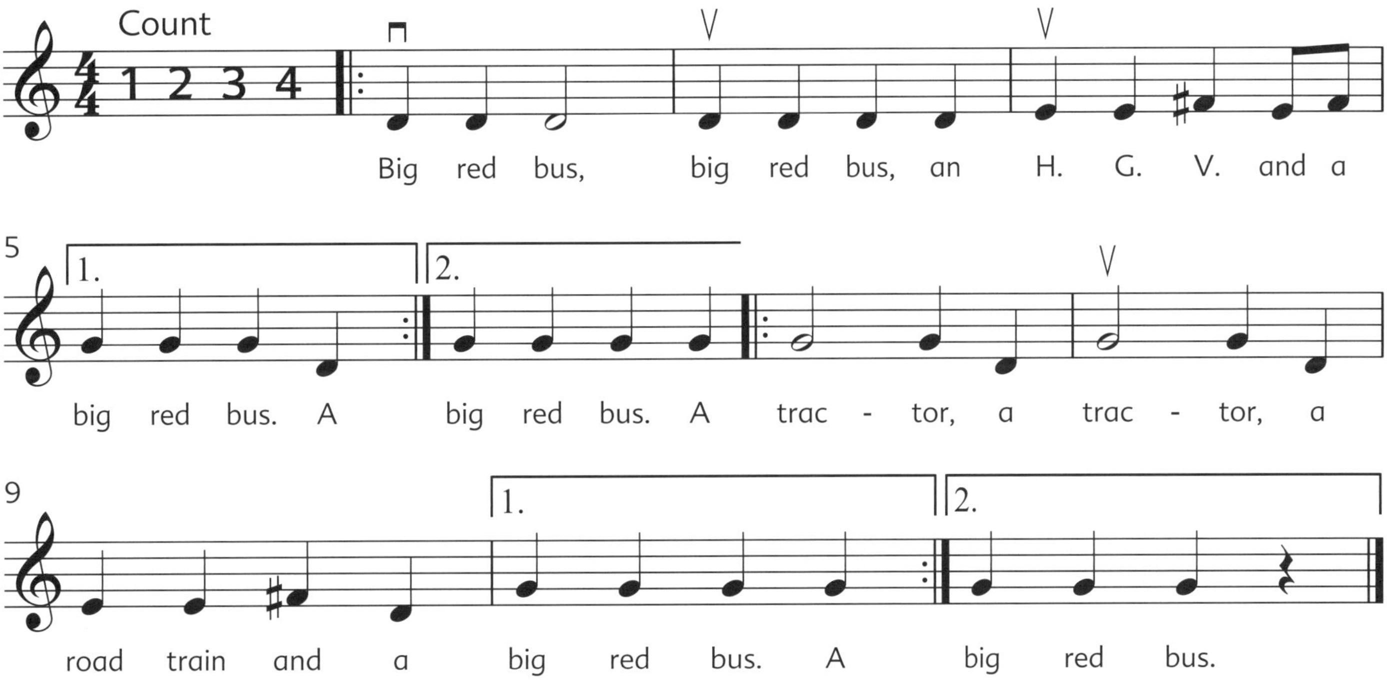

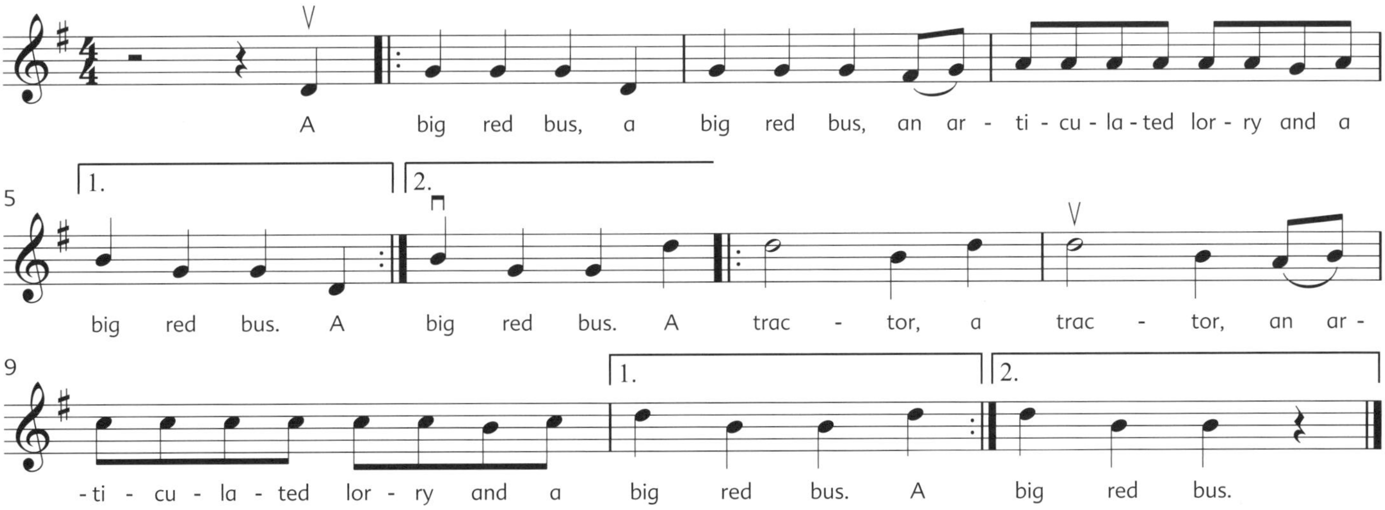

Count
1 2 3 4
Big red bus, big red bus, an H. G. V. and a
5
1.
2.
big red bus. A big red bus. A trac - tor, a trac - tor, a
9
1.
2.
road train and a big red bus. A big red bus.

A big red bus, a big red bus, an ar - ti - cu - la - ted lor - ry and a
5
1.
2.
big red bus. A big red bus. A trac - tor, a trac - tor, an ar -
9
1.
2.
- ti - cu - la - ted lor - ry and a big red bus. A big red bus.

21 Ostinato accompaniment for ***Clown dance***

1.
2.

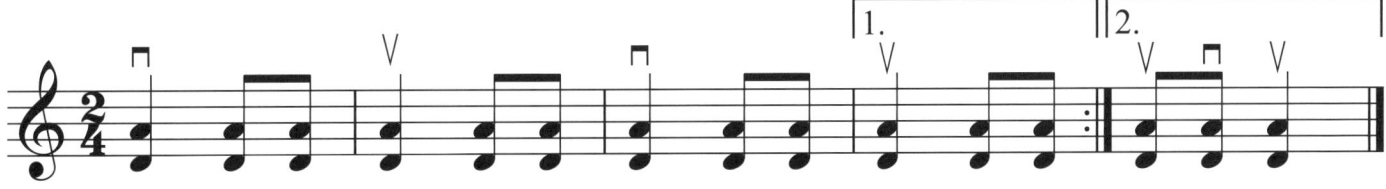

D.C. al Fine tells you to repeat the music from the beginning up to **Fine**. **D.C.** is short for **Da Capo**, meaning from the beginning. **Fine** means 'end'.

This piece begins on G, played with the 3rd finger. Make sure the G is in tune before you start the piece. Climb up to it by playing D (open), then E (1st finger), then F♯ (2nd finger), then G (3rd finger).

23 Au clair de la lune (48-49)

traditional French

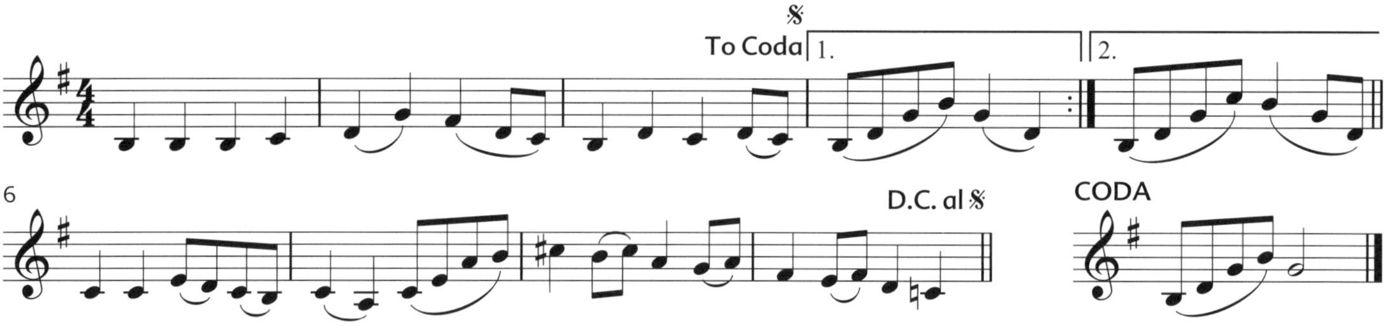

Play *Twinkle, twinkle little bow* twice – fast the first time and slowly the second time.

Hum the melody while your teacher plays the accompaniment. Watch your teacher's bowing action, especially in the middle section.

24 Twinkle, twinkle little bow (50-51)

words JS, music traditional

(pupil's part)

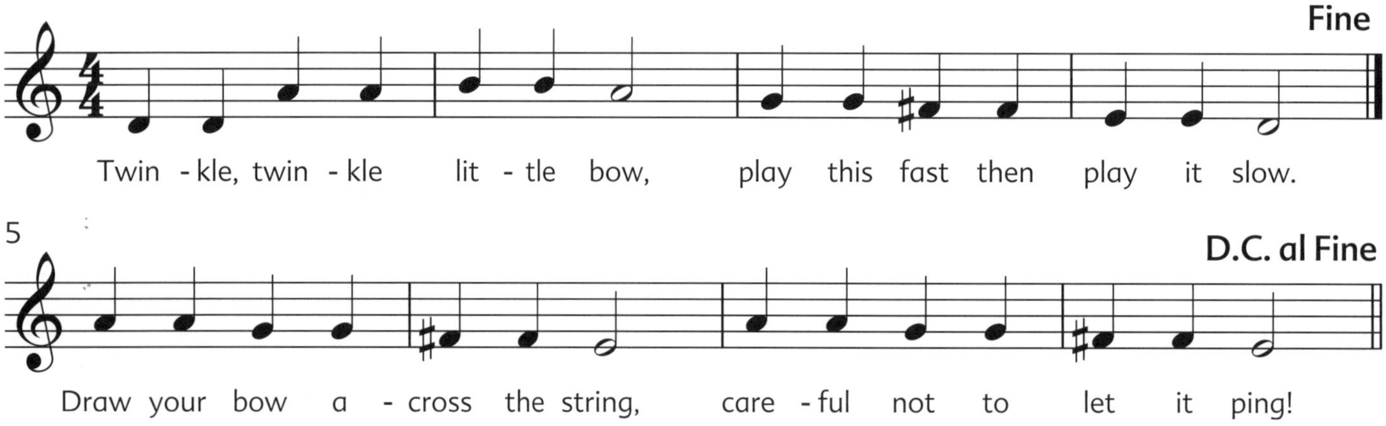

Twin - kle, twin - kle lit - tle bow, play this fast then play it slow.

Draw your bow a - cross the string, care - ful not to let it ping!

25 Miss Mary Mac

52-53

traditional

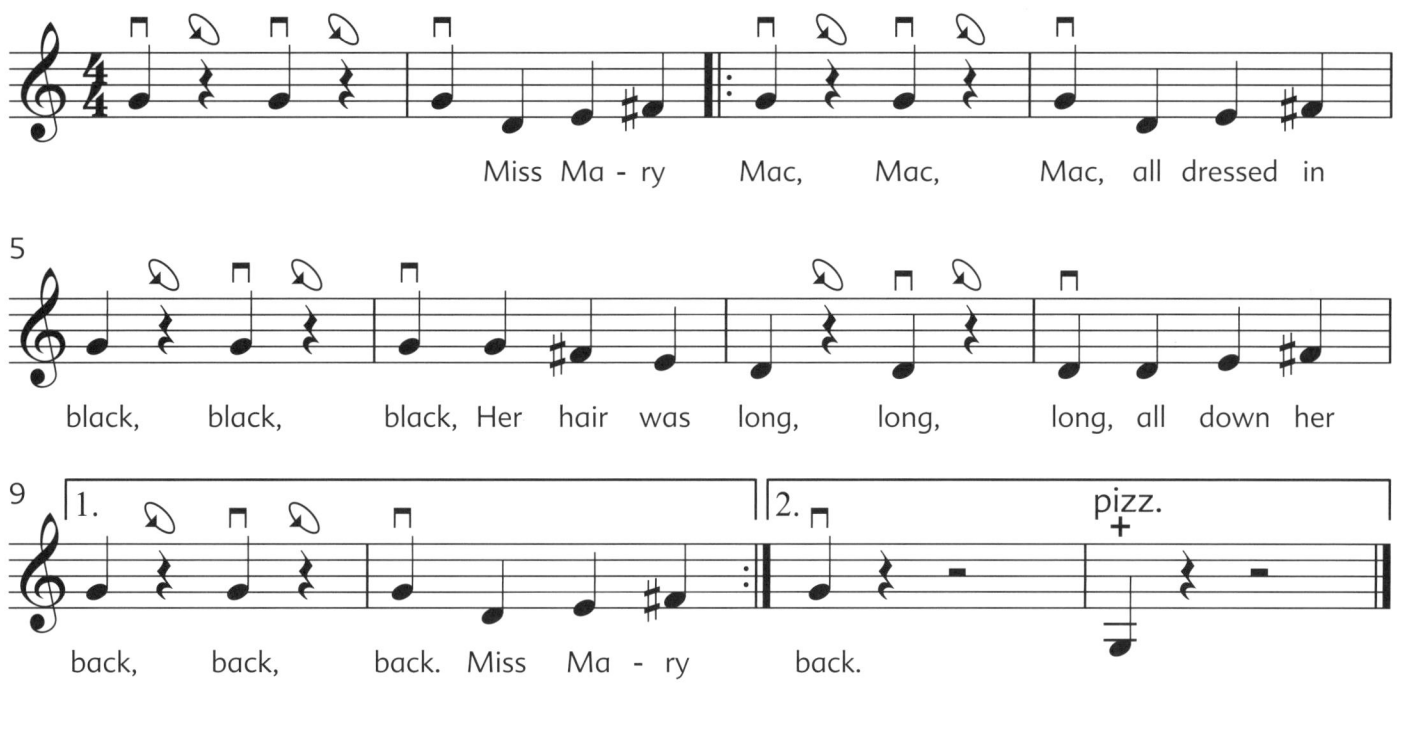

24 Twinkle, twinkle little bow

(teacher's part)

Not all tunes begin on the first beat of the bar. Some start on the last beat of the bar, the **upbeat**. An **upbeat** is usually played with an up-bow.

When a piece begins on an **upbeat**, the final bar has one less beat than usual so that there are the correct number of beats in the piece.

Play the next song over and over without pausing in between. Find a way to end the piece. Then play it again, starting slowly and gradually getting faster each time.

26 The song that never stops (duet)  CH

27 Whistle while you work (duet)

words Larry Morey, music Frank Churchill

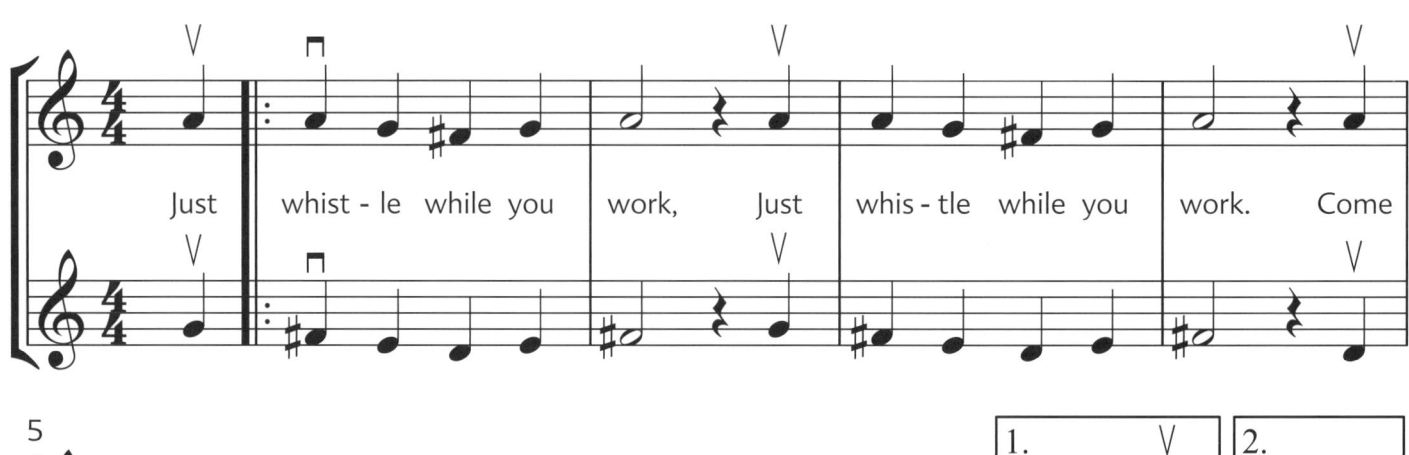

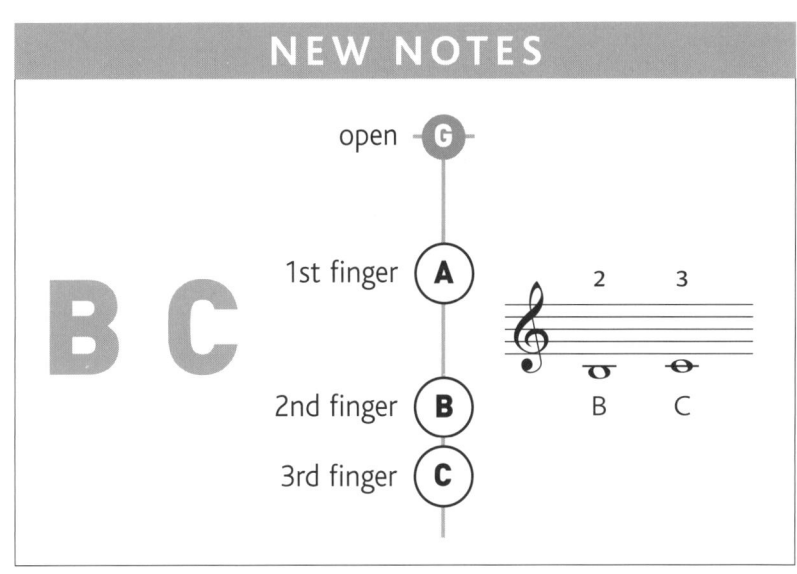

 A **key signature** is written at the beginning of each line. This is the key signature for **G major**, in which all Fs are sharp (♯).

28 Secret agents (duet)

words JS, music traditional

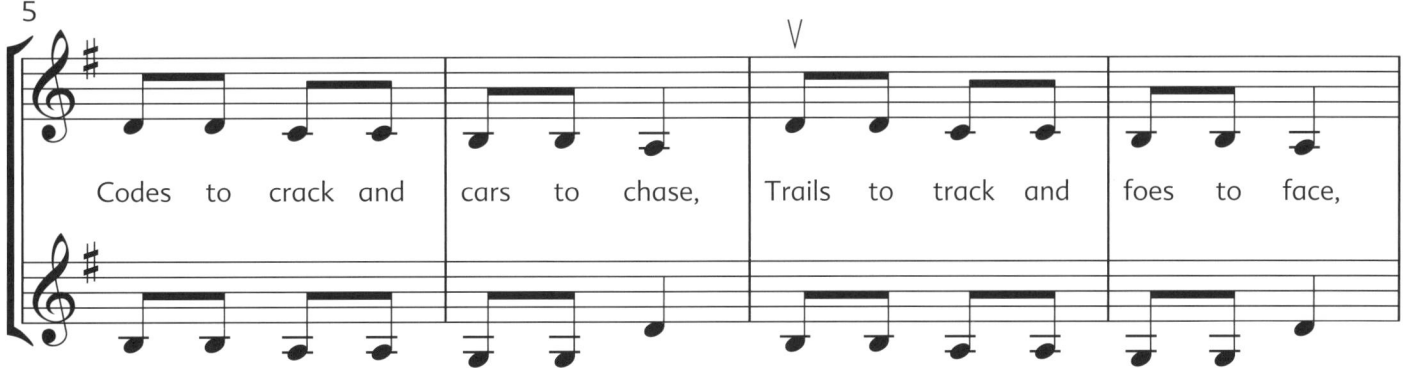
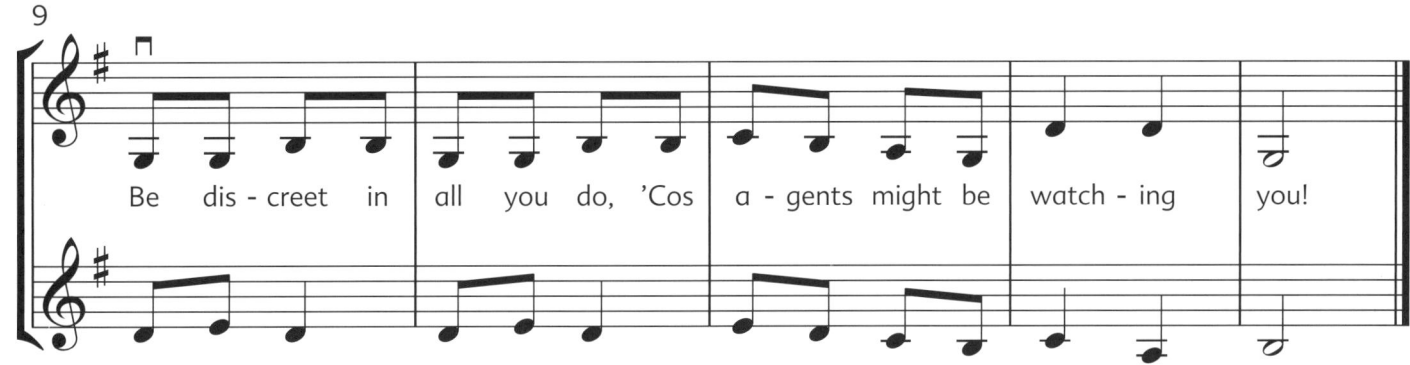

D.S. al Fine tells you to repeat the music from 𝄋 up to **Fine**. **D.S.** is short for **Dal Segno**, meaning 'from the sign'.

𝅝 **semibreve** – worth four crotchet beats.

s.b. is short for 'slow bow'. Use the whole of your bow to play any note marked s.b.

(⊓) tells you to play a down-bow on the repeat.

29 Little bird (60-61)

traditional German

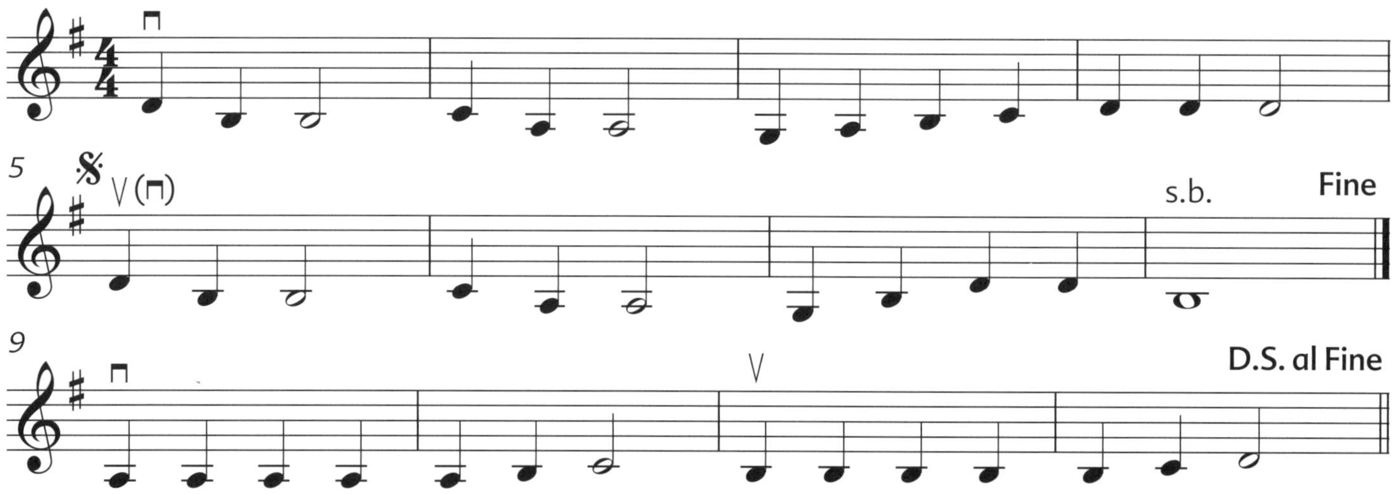

5
s.b.
Fine
9
D.S. al Fine

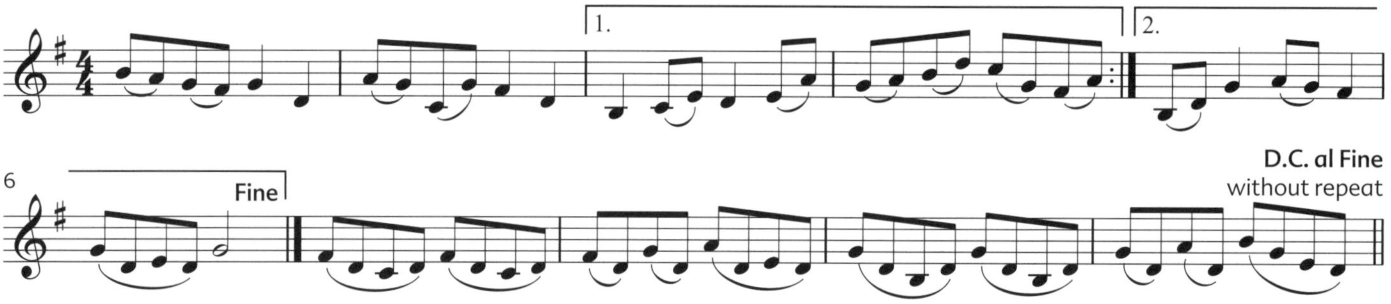

1.
2.
6
Fine
D.C. al Fine
without repeat

30 Summer shine (duet) (62-63)

words CH, music PD

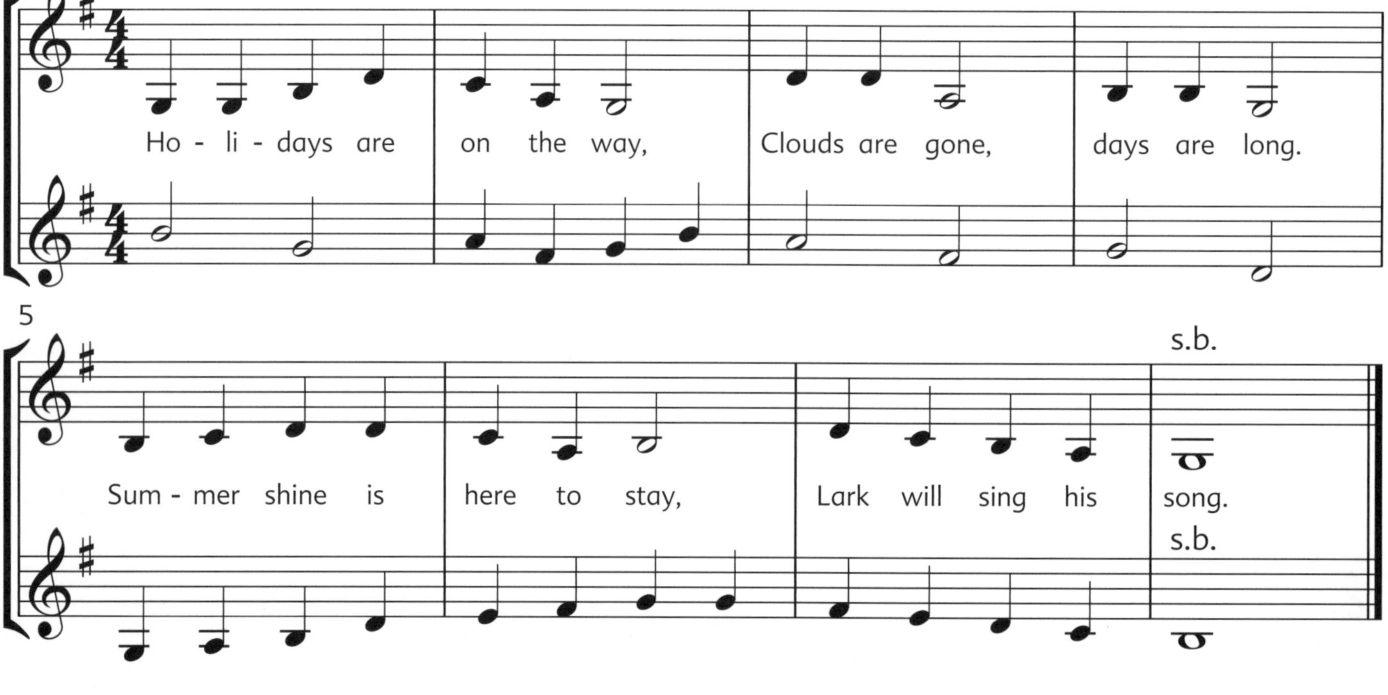

Ho - li - days are on the way, Clouds are gone, days are long.
5
s.b.
Sum - mer shine is here to stay, Lark will sing his song.
s.b.

Play ***Summer shine*** at the same speed as before, but play each note twice:

♩ becomes ♫   𝅗𝅥 becomes ♩ ♩

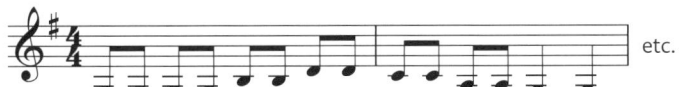

Use the middle of the bow to play the quavers and keep your bowing wrist relaxed.

etc.

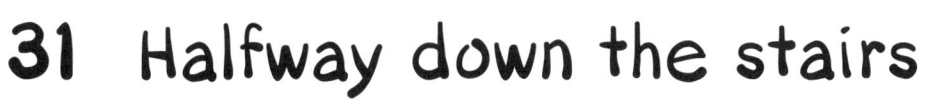

31 Halfway down the stairs

64-65

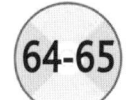

words A A Milne,
music H Fraser Simson

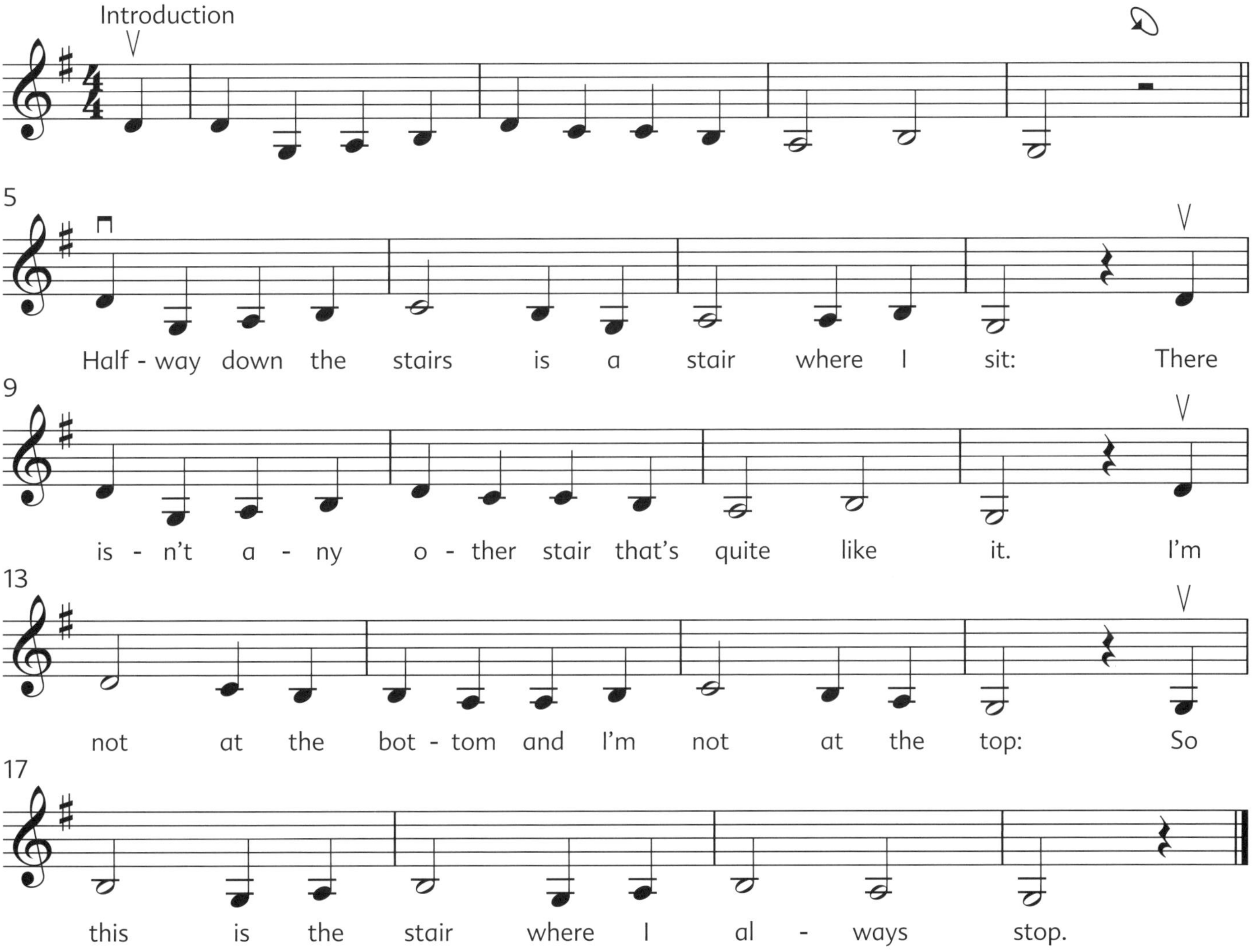
Introduction
5
Half - way down the stairs is a stair where I sit: There
9
is - n't a - ny o - ther stair that's quite like it. I'm
13
not at the bot - tom and I'm not at the top: So
17
this is the stair where I al - ways stop.

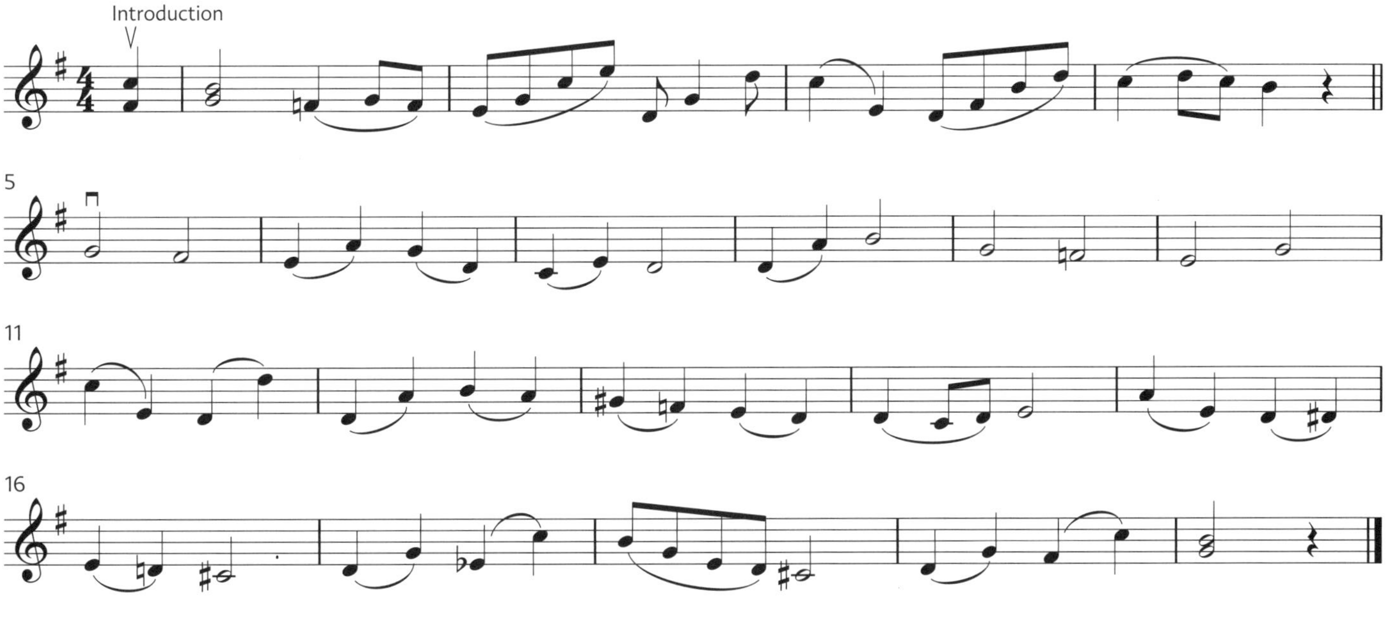
Introduction
5
11
16

32 Old MacDonald 66-67

words adapted by SR, music traditional

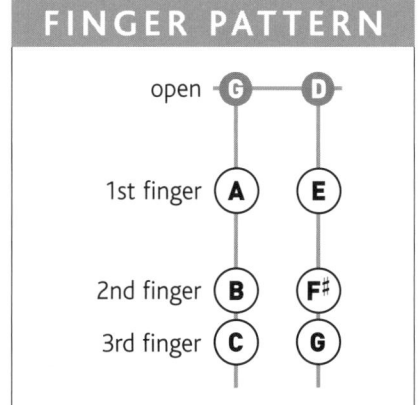

 Here is the scale of G major.
The key signature is one sharp: F#.

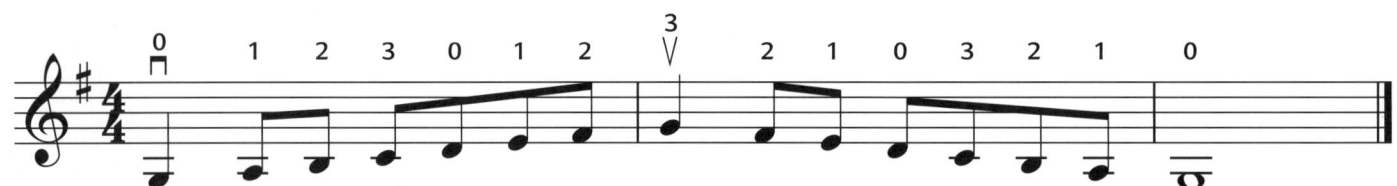

step 7

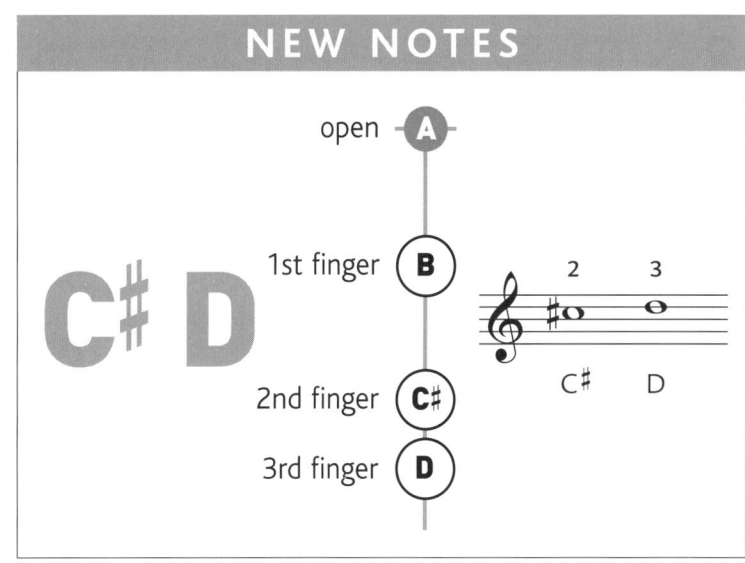

 This is the key signature for **D major**, in which all Fs and Cs are sharp (♯).

An instruction such as **Cheerfully** at the beginning of a piece tells you about the character of the music and how fast or slow it should be played.

These instructions are usually written in English or Italian. To find out what the Italian terms mean, look at the **glossary** at the back of the book.

Try playing the accompaniment to *Brown bread* pizzicato.

33 Brown bread (duet)

CH

34 Big Ben (duet)

traditional

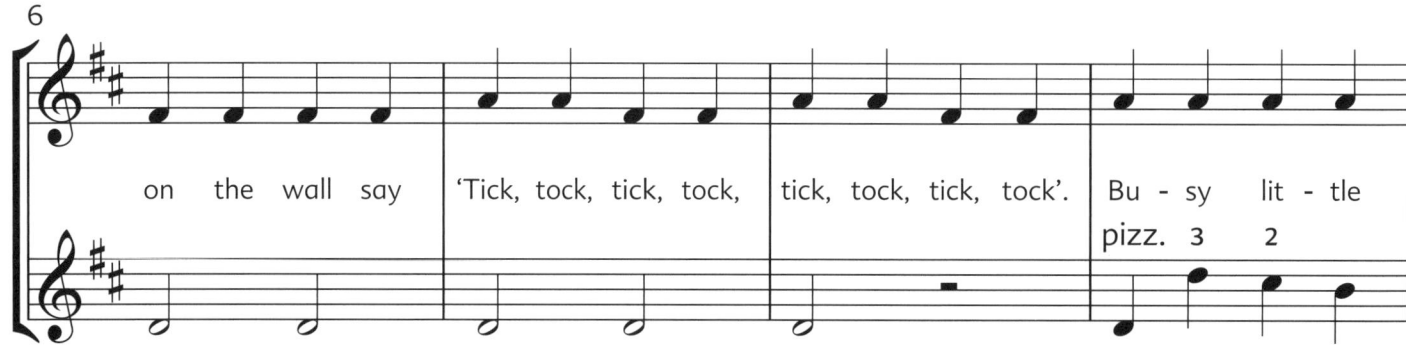

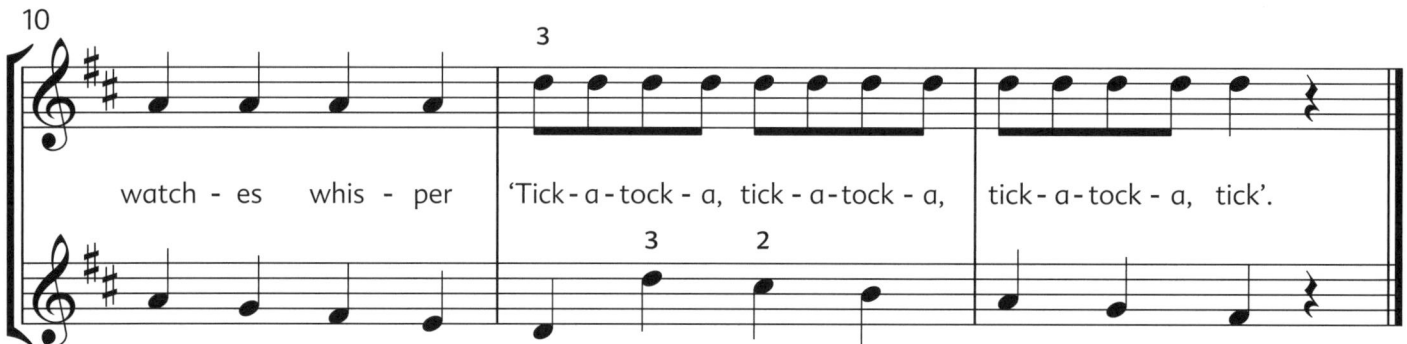

 A **round** is a piece of music in which two or more people play or sing the same tune but start at different times. **Allegro** – fast and lively.

35 Turn the glasses over (round)

traditional

* entry point when played as a round

36 Off to France in the morning

words CH, music PD

Brightly

Off to France, just for a day, Glad that it's not too far a-way.

Get-ting up at the crack of the dawn, When ev-'ry-one is yawn-ing.

Off on the train and I hope it won't rain, We'll sing out a song as we roll a-long.

I can't wait, let's ce-le-brate, 'Cos we're off to France in the morn-ing.

 Here is the scale of D major. The key signature is two sharps: F♯ and C♯.

To practise reading in D major, play your teacher's part in no. 7 *Little playmates*.

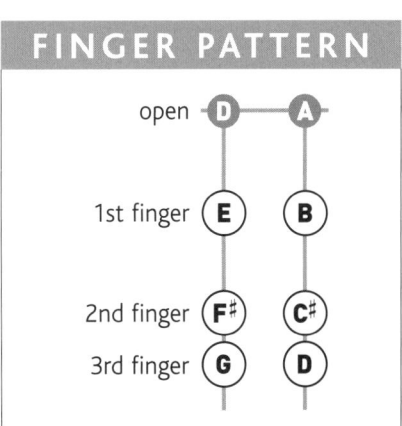

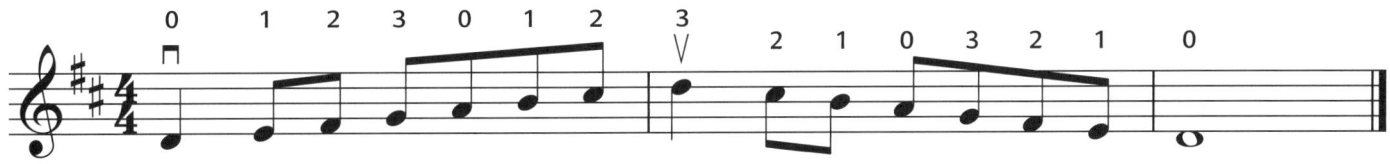

step 8

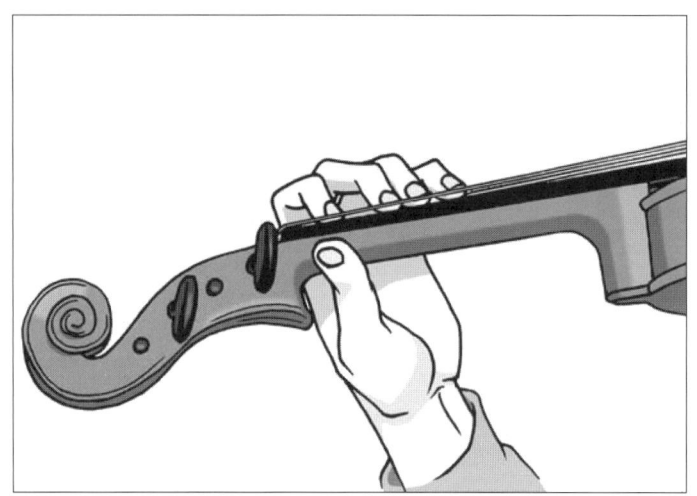

NEW NOTE

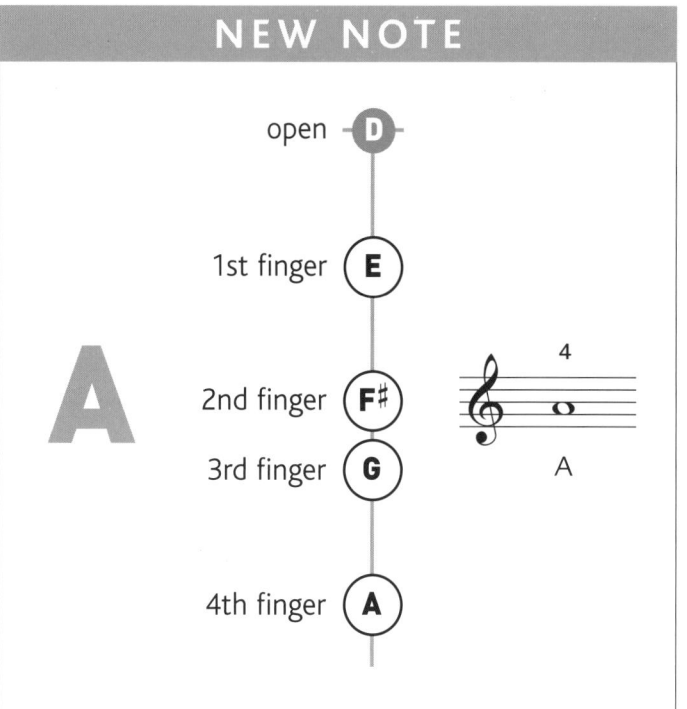

 You can use either the open string or your **4th finger** to play the note A. The choice you make will depend on the notes before and after the note A.

In the following pieces the fingering is marked.

Do you recognise the tune of *Racing Driver*? (Look at no.15.)

Try playing this tune by ear, starting on the A string.

37 Racing driver (round) 76-77

words CH, music traditional French

Ra - cing dri - ver, ra - cing dri - ver, In your car, in your car,

Fill it up with pet - rol, fill it up with pet - rol, You'll go far, you'll go far.

* entry point when played as a round

Andante – at a leisurely pace.

38 Long, long ago (duet)

78-79

Thomas H Bayly

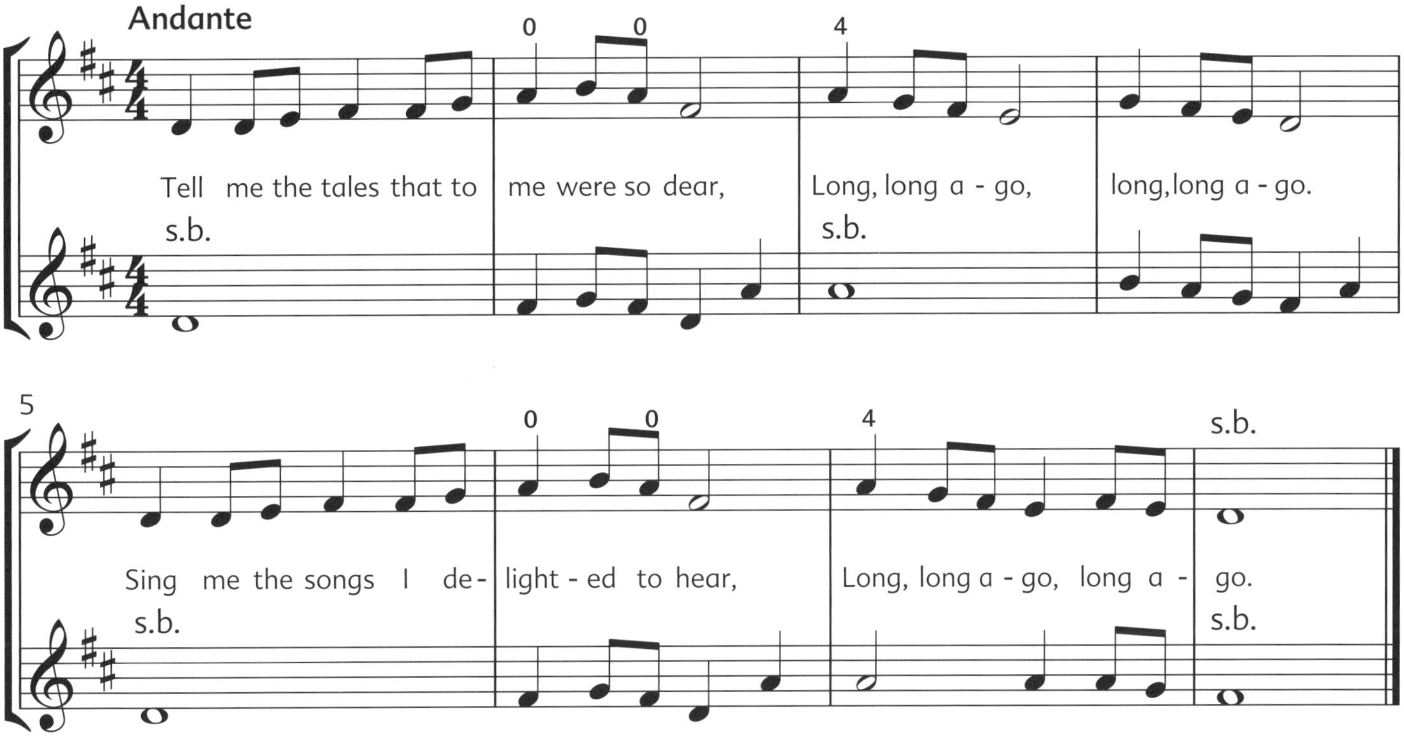
Andante
0 0 4
Tell me the tales that to me were so dear, Long, long a - go, long, long a - go.
s.b. s.b.
5
0 0 4 s.b.
Sing me the songs I de- light - ed to hear, Long, long a - go, long a - go.
s.b. s.b.

39 Ode to joy (duet)

80-81

Ludwig van Beethoven

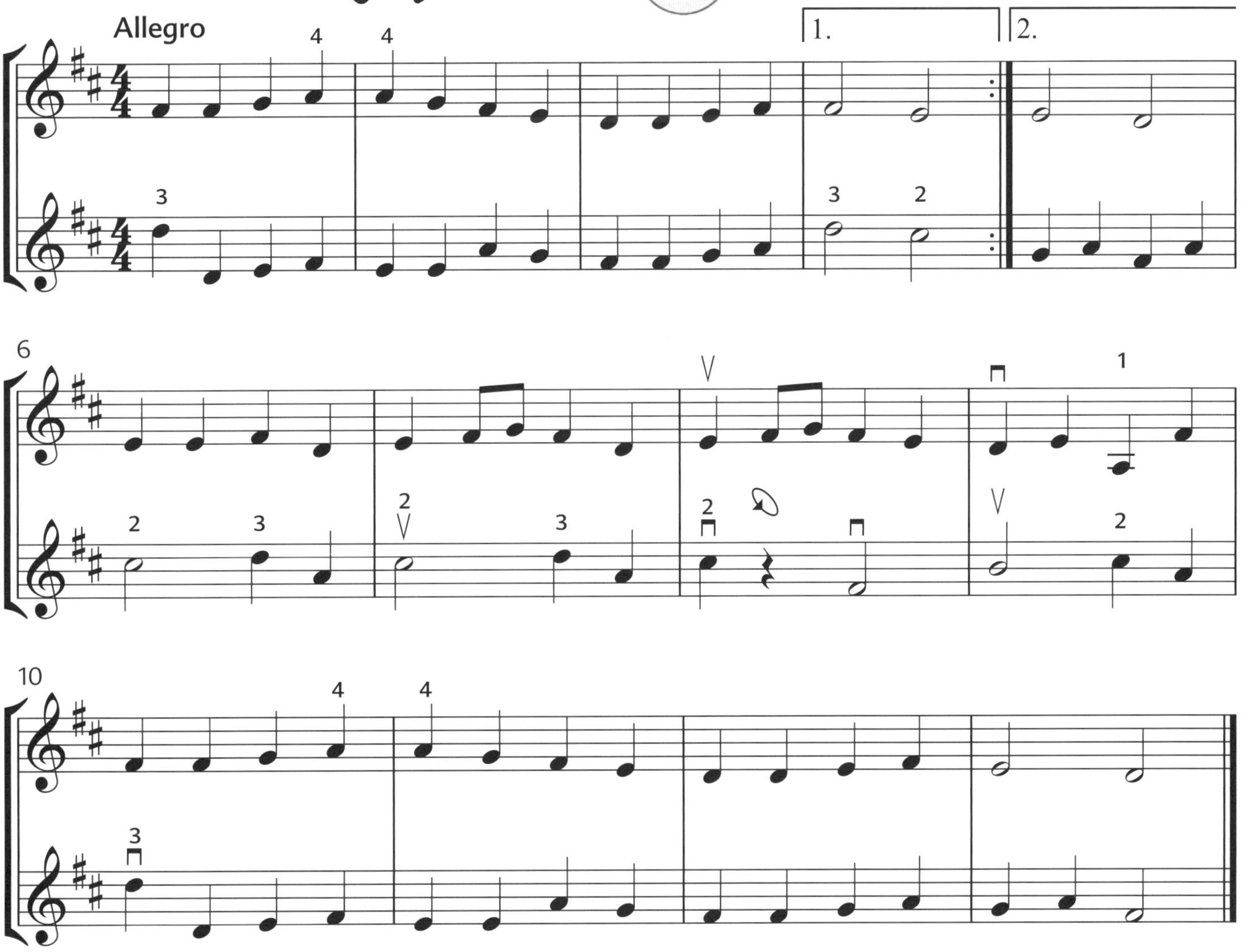
Allegro
4 4
1. 2.
3
3 2
6
1
2 3
2
3
2
2
10
4 4
3

 **semibreve rest** – lasts for four crotchet beats of silence.

Cantabile – in a singing style.

40 The way you look tonight

Jerome Kern

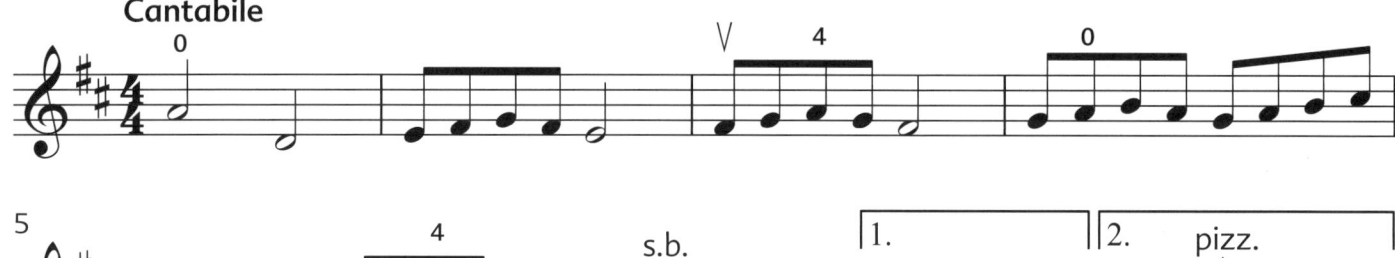

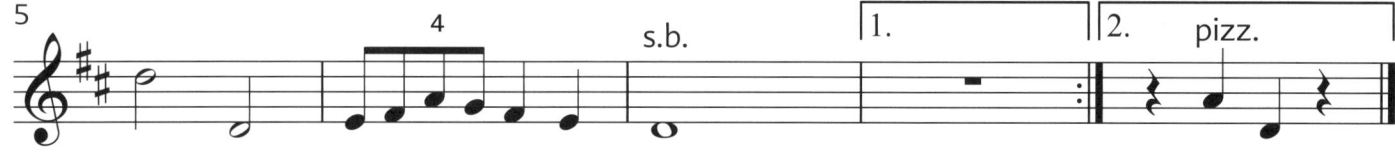

41 (Meet the) Flintstones

(teacher's part)

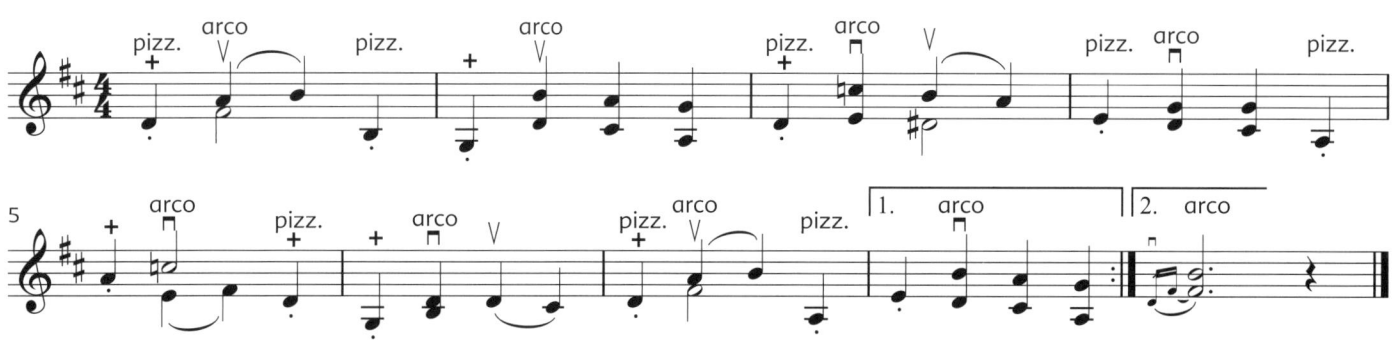

 Aim to play this tune quickly, but practise slowly at first. Notice that there is a rest on the first beat of some bars.

41 (Meet the) Flintstones

Joseph Barbera, William Hanna and Hoyt Curtin

(pupil's part)

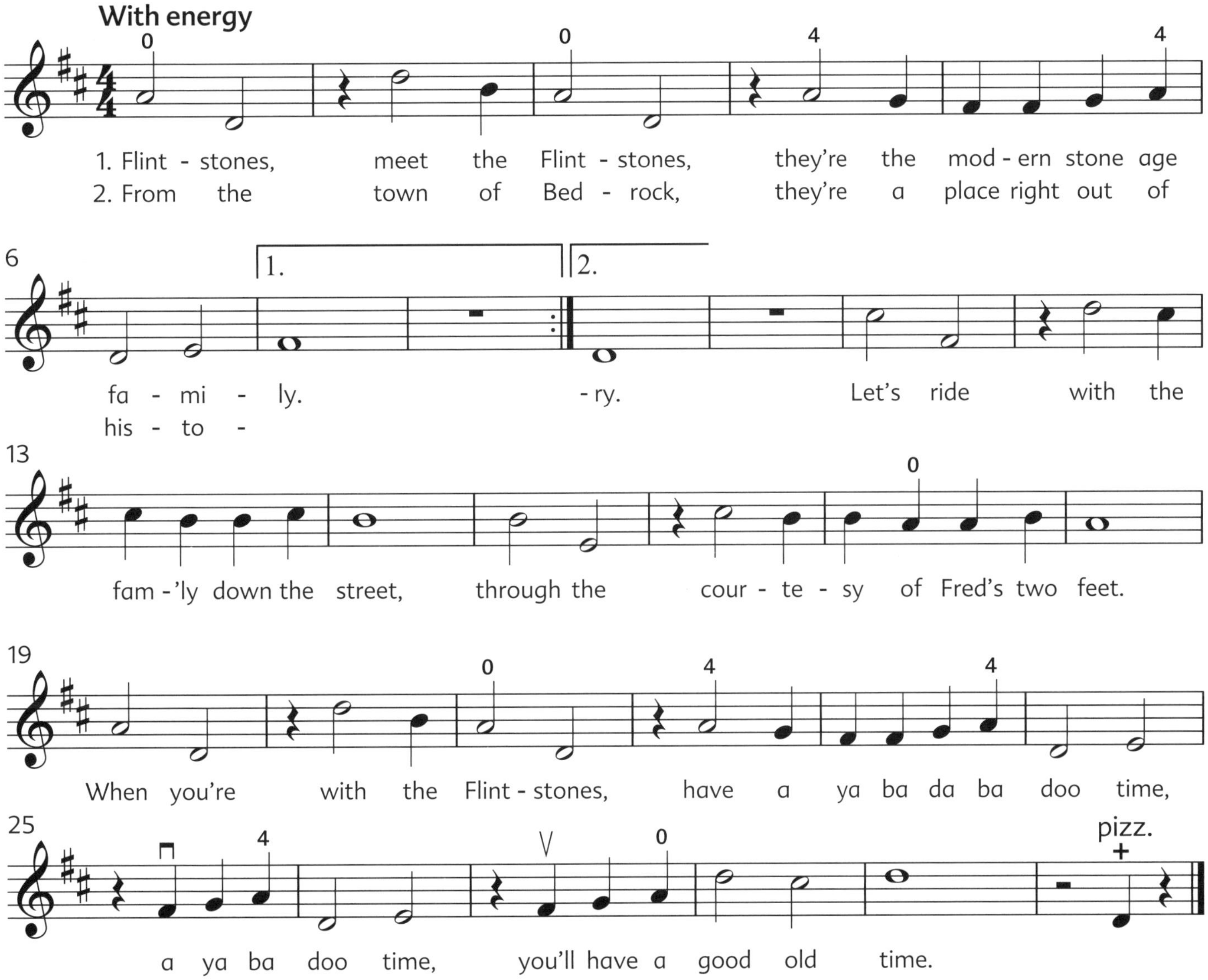

With energy

1. Flint - stones, meet the Flint - stones, they're the mod - ern stone age fa - mi - ly.
2. From the town of Bed - rock, they're a place right out of his - to - ry.

Let's ride with the fam - 'ly down the street, through the cour - te - sy of Fred's two feet.

When you're with the Flint - stones, have a ya ba da ba doo time, a ya ba doo time, you'll have a good old time.

step 9

A **slur** joins two notes of different pitch and is played in one bow, which enables you to play smoothly.

The Italian term for playing smoothly is **legato**.

42 I came from Alabama

traditional North American, arr. CH

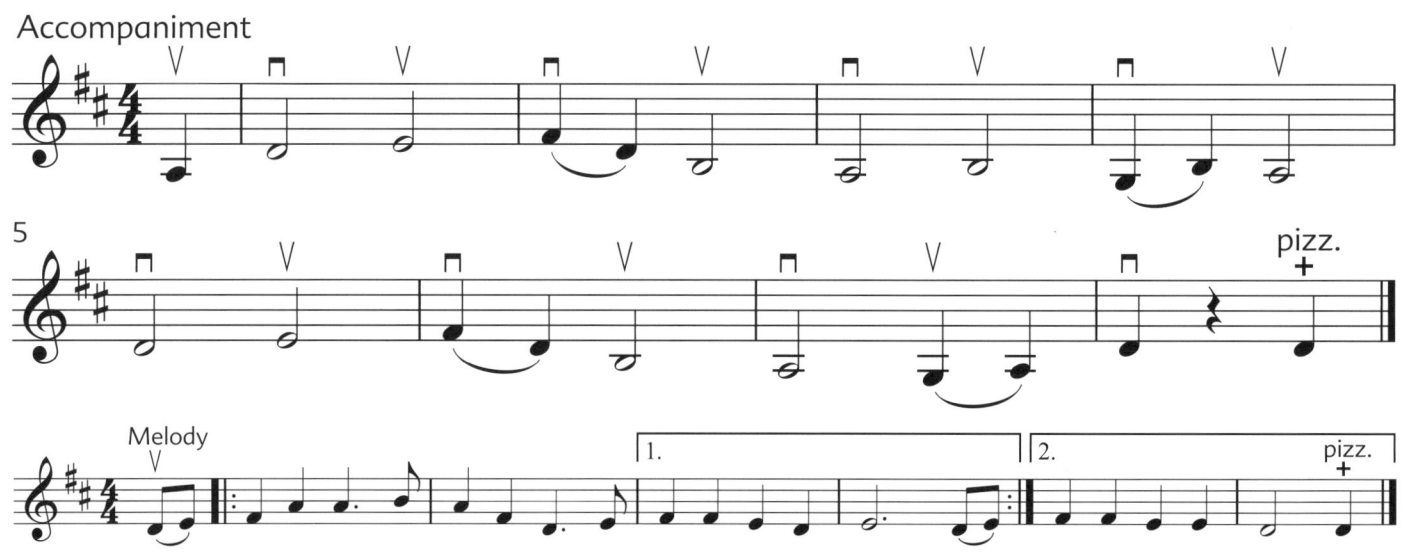

43 Morningtown ride

Malvina Reynolds

44 Troika 90-91

Sergei Prokofiev

45 Daydreamer 92-93

CH

Think how day-dreams soothe, when all the ed-ges blur. To make the mu-sic smooth, then join notes with a slur.

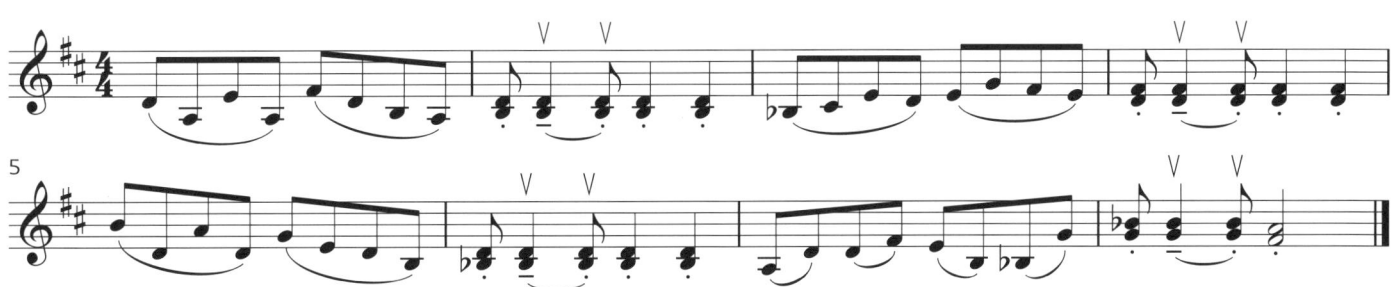

43 Morningtown ride (teacher's part continued)

step 10

 **3/4** This time signature shows that there are three crotchet beats in each bar.

dotted minim – worth three crotchet beats.

A dot after a note makes it last longer by adding half the value of the original note.   2 + 1 = 3

46 Roses from the South

Johann Strauss II

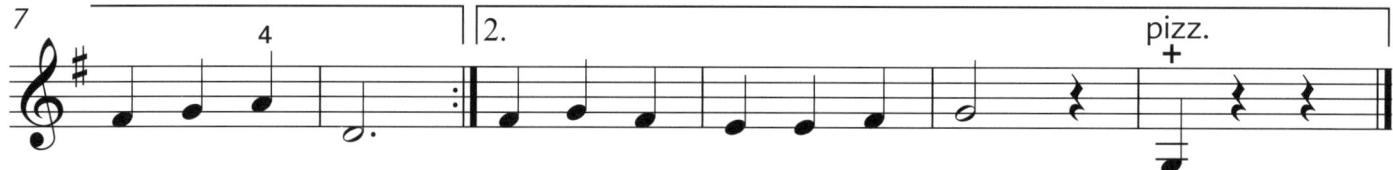

Your friend

Your teacher

 Dolce – sweetly.

47 Lavender's blue (duet)

traditional

La - ven - der's   blue, dil - ly, dil - ly,   La - ven - der's   green;

Two notes joined by a **tie** make one note which lasts the length of both notes.

Tied notes are played in one bow.

48 Call of the carousel

CH

step 11

 In this step you will practise a slow-fast bowing pattern in $\frac{3}{4}$

Dynamics tell you how quietly or loudly to play.

p tells you to play quietly. It stands for **piano**, meaning 'quiet';

f tells you to play loudly. It stands for **forte**, meaning 'loud'.

49 We all stand together (duet)

Paul McCartney

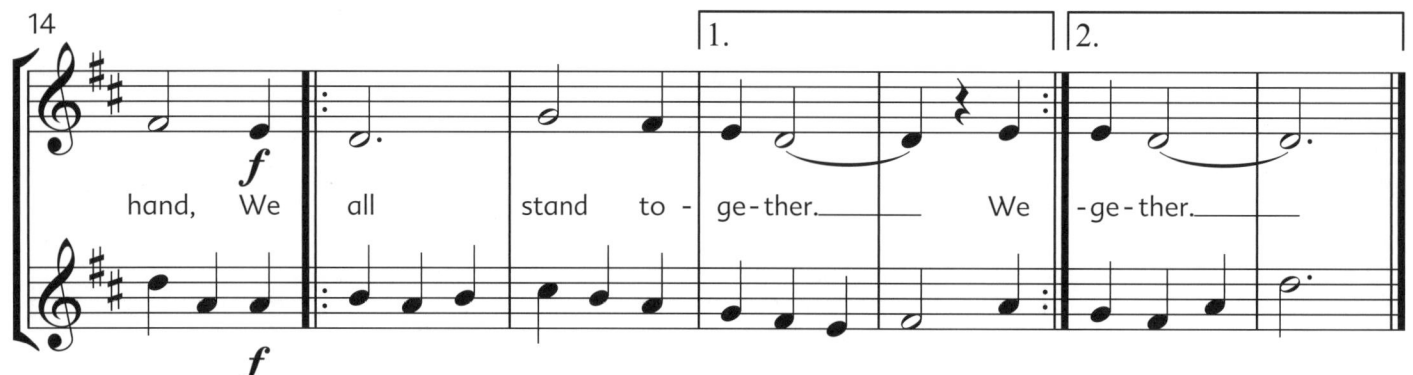

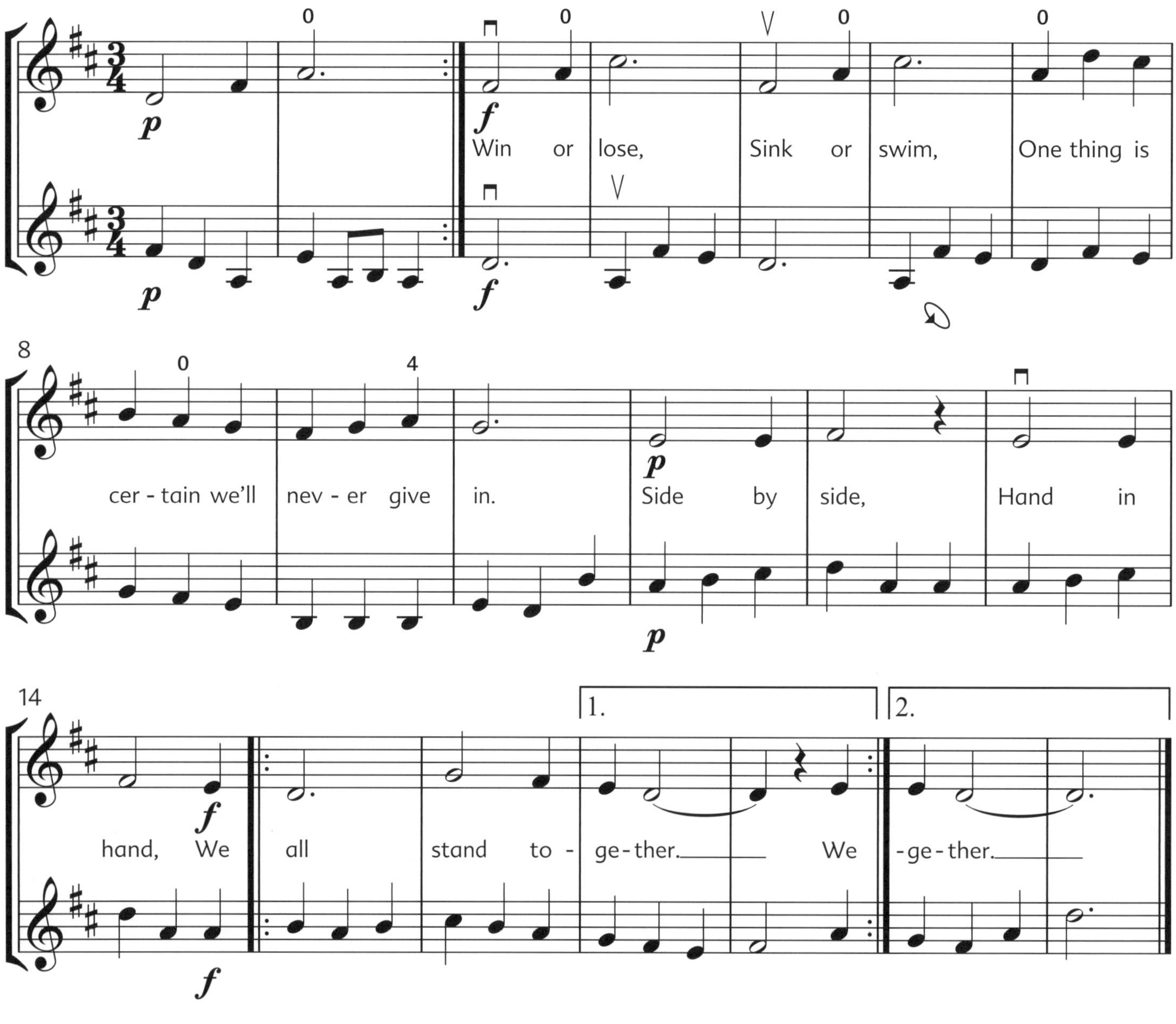

Espressivo – expressively.

50 Edelweiss

words Oscar Hammerstein II, music Richard Rodgers

Espressivo

p E - del - weiss, E - del - weiss, Ev - 'ry morn - ing you greet me. Small and white, Clean and bright, You look hap - py to meet me. *f* Blos - som of snow, may you bloom and grow, Bloom and grow for ev - er. *p* E - del - weiss, E - del - weiss, Bless my home - land for ev - er.

 ♮ is a **natural sign**. It cancels the effect of a sharp.

51 On top of Old Smokey (duet)

traditional North American

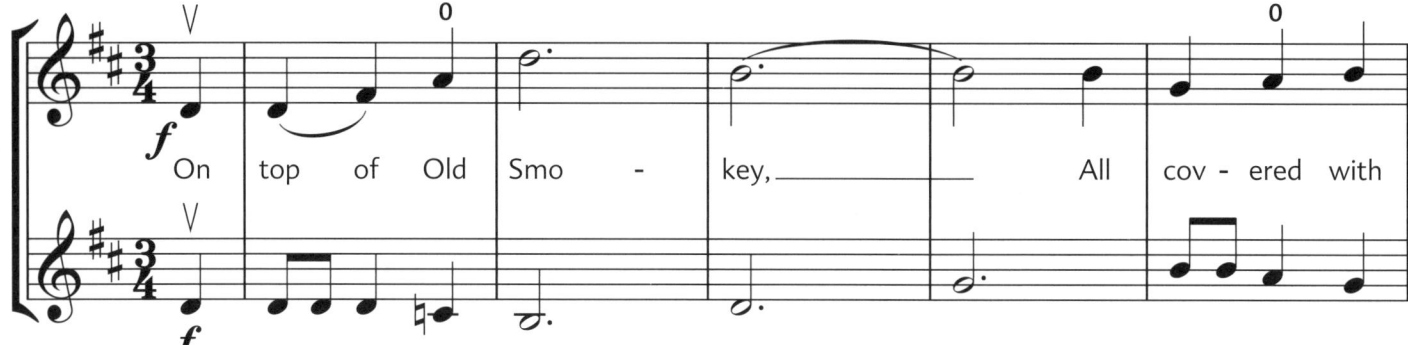
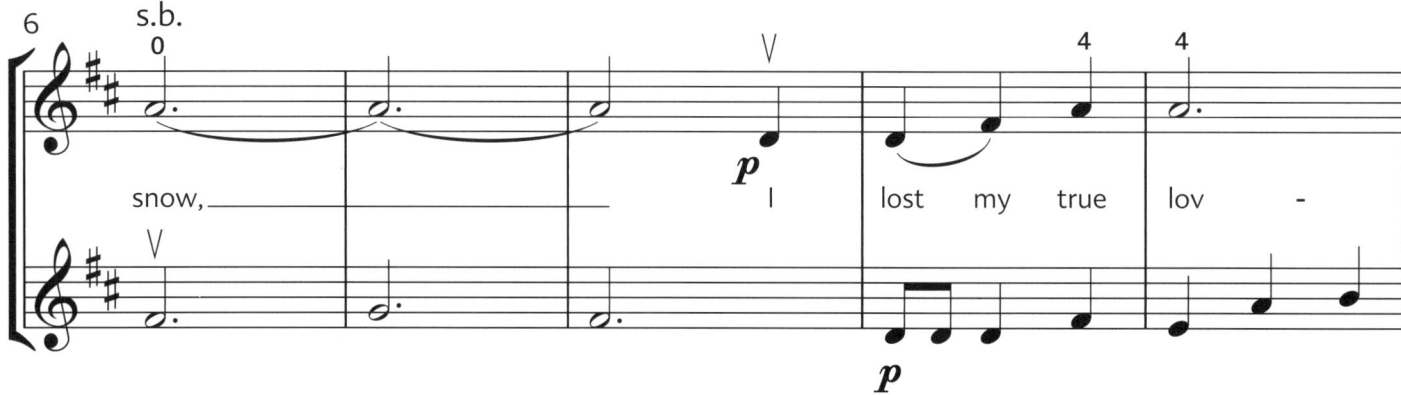
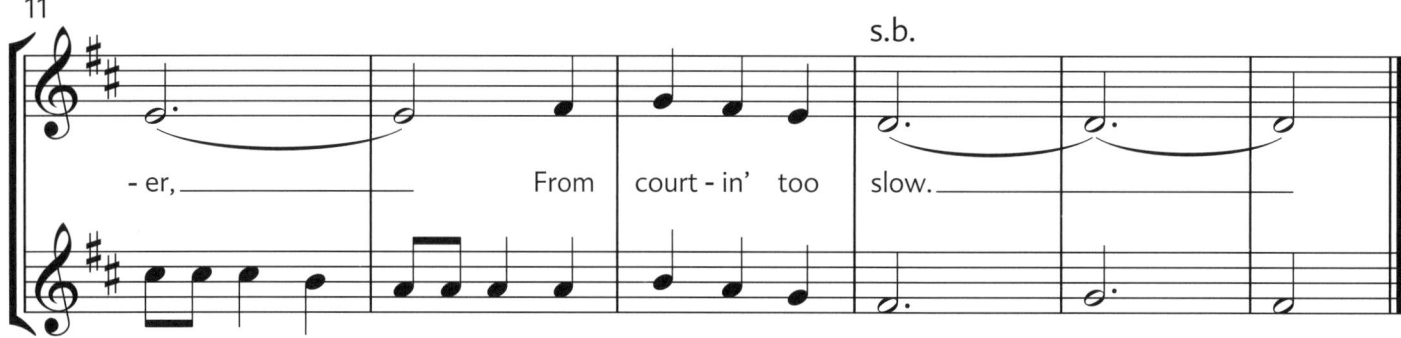

 Con fuoco – with fire.

Play *London's burning* twice: 1st time *p*   2nd time *f*

52 London's burning (round)

traditional

✱ entry point when played as a round

53 The hippopotamus song

14-15

words Michael Flanders,
music Donald Swann

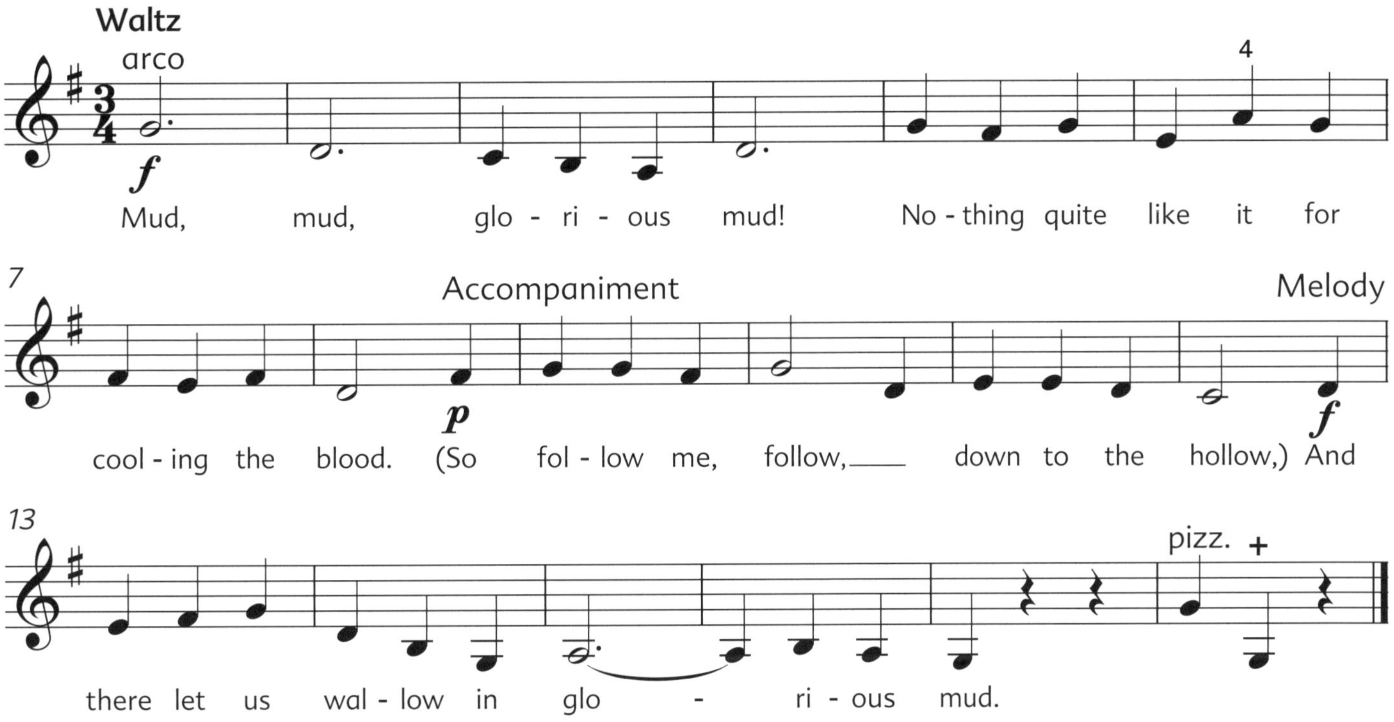

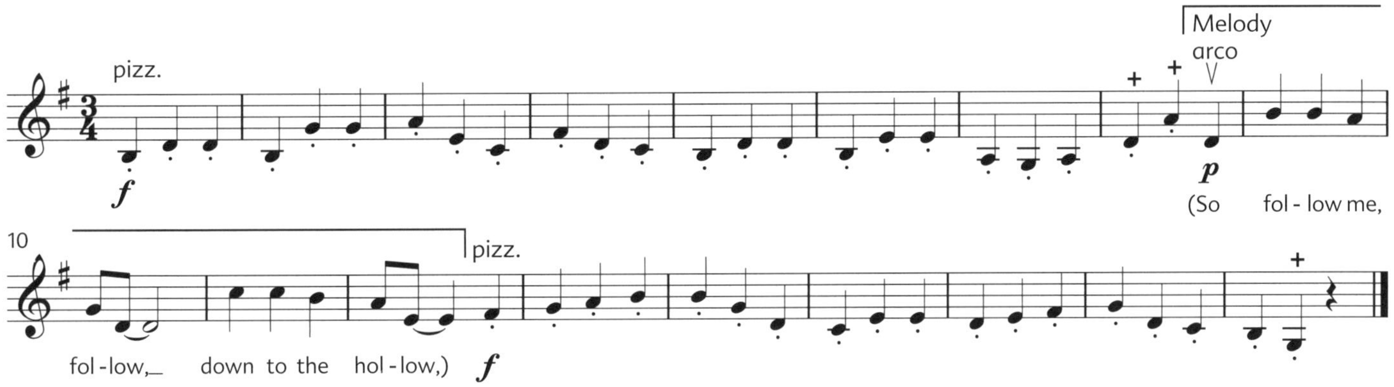

step 12

⭐ ♩. **dotted crotchet** – worth one and a half crotchet beats:

These two rhythms look different, but sound the same:

f.b. – fast bow.

54 London Bridge (duet)

traditional

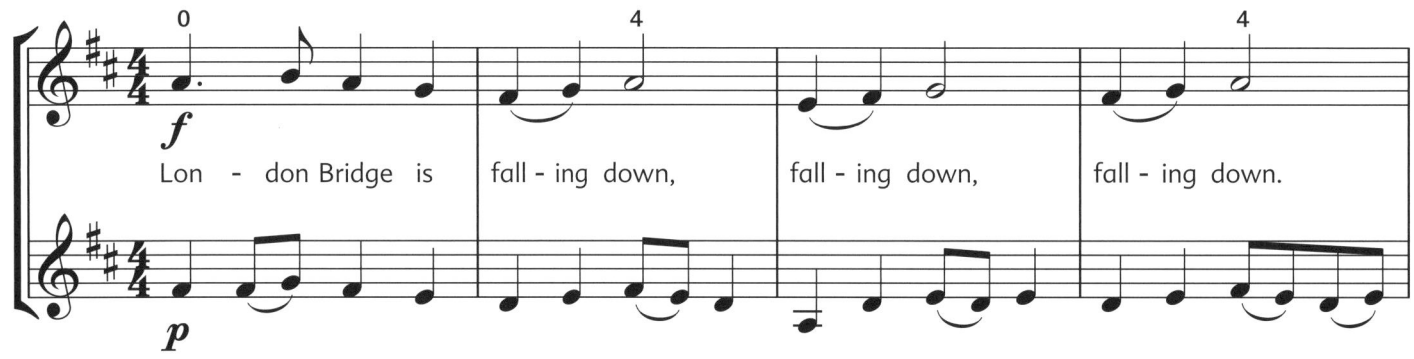

⭐ **Leggiero** – lightly.

55 Tea for two (pupil's part)

words Irving Caesar,
music Vincent Youmans, arr. CH

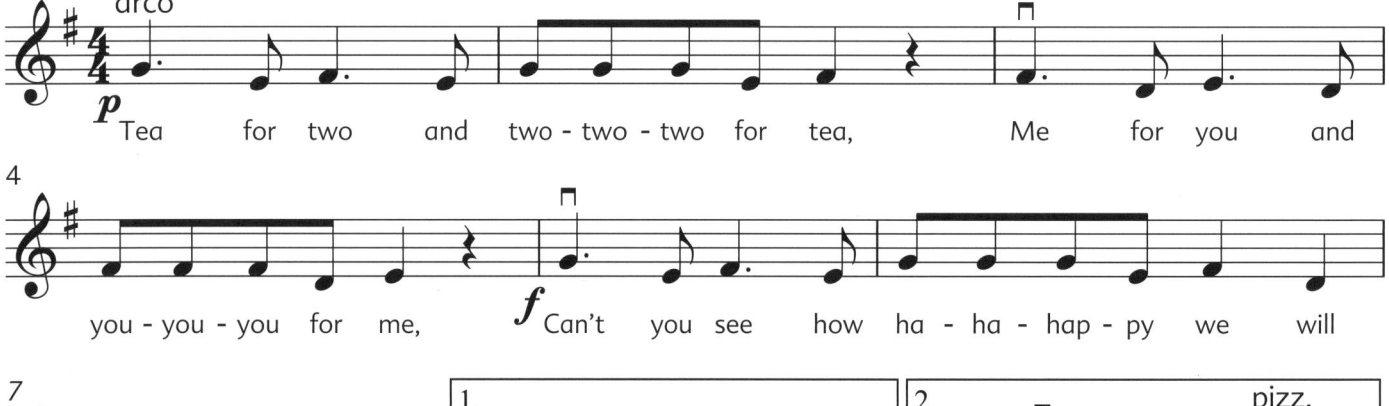
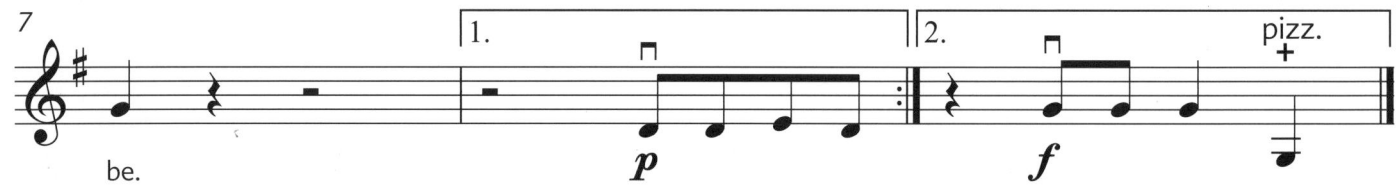

To practise dotted rhythms, play your teacher's part in

no. 42 *I came from Alabama*
no. 4 *When the saints go marching in*
no. 6 *A-tisket, a-tasket*

56 Stand by me

20-21

Ben E King, Jerry Leiber and Mike Stoller, arr. CH

Rhythmically

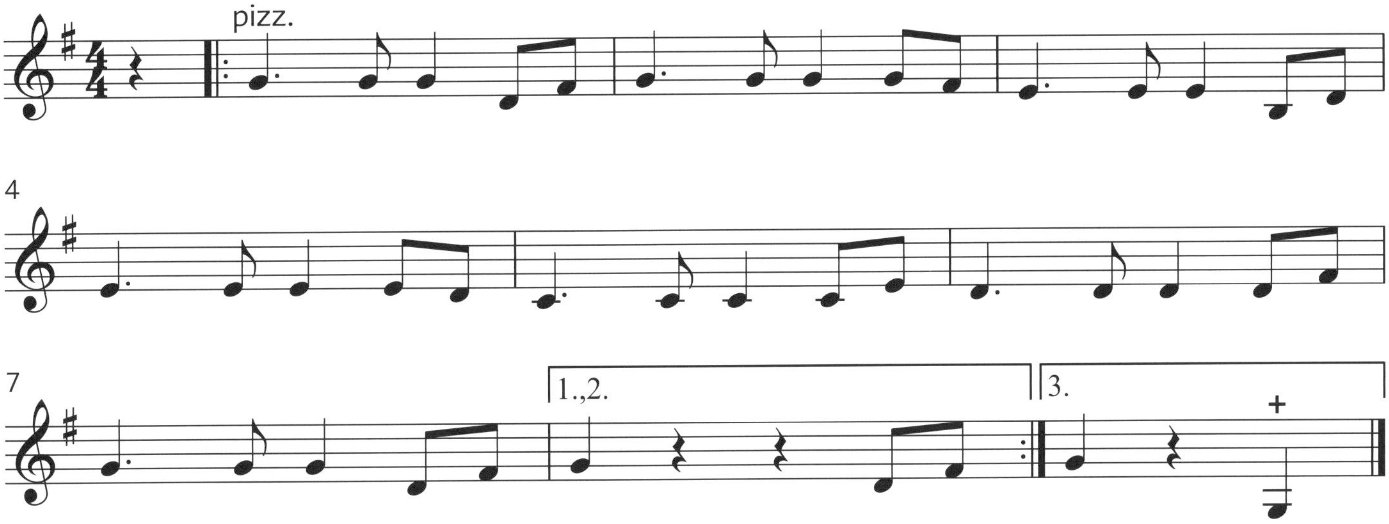

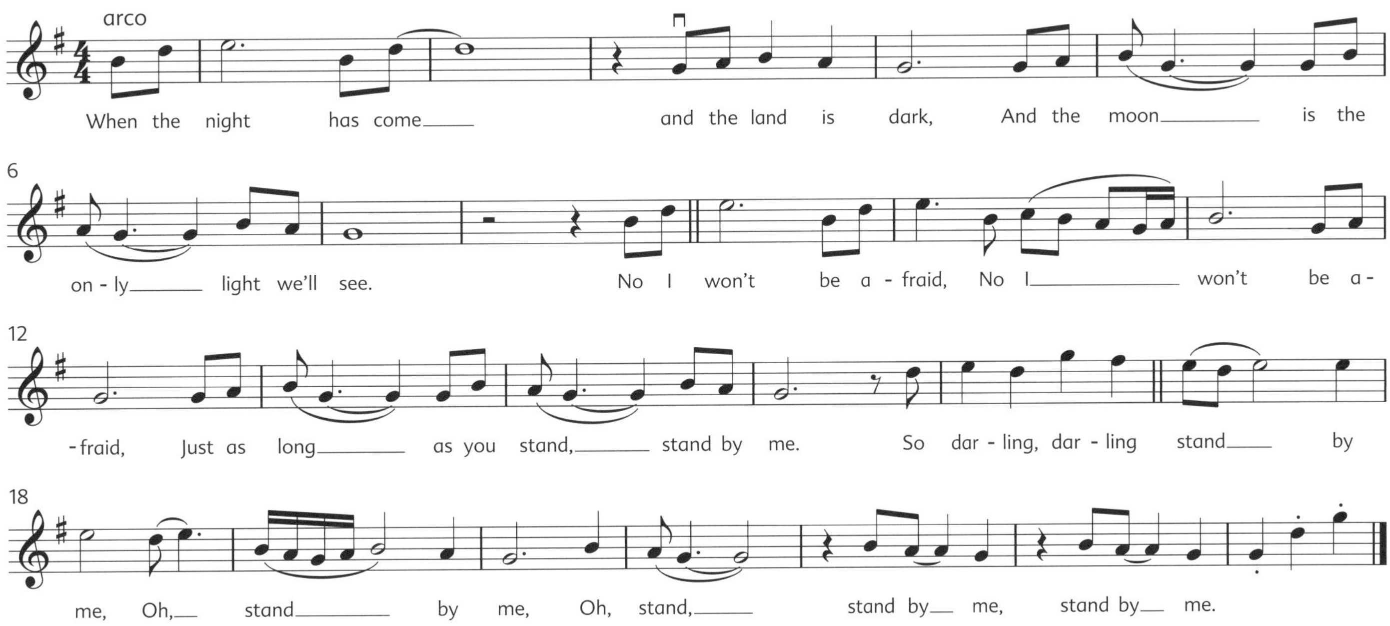

55 Tea for two (teacher's part)

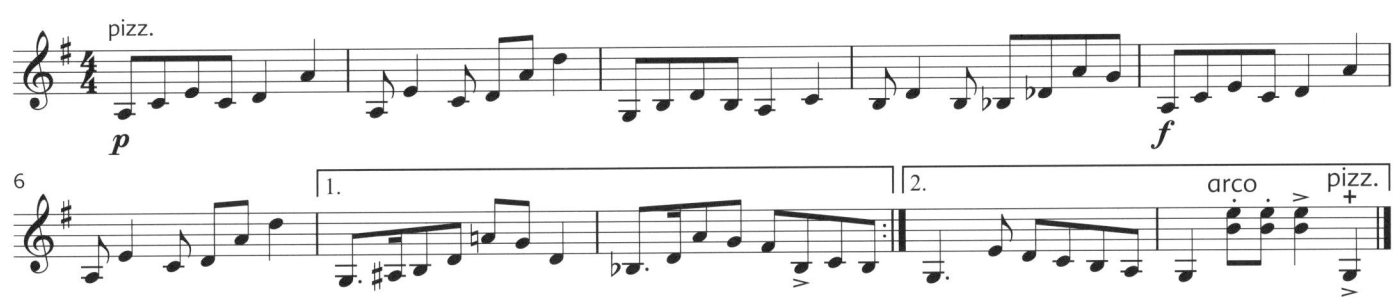

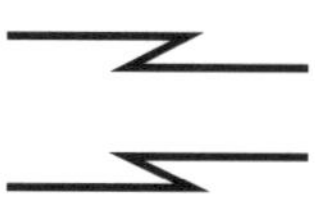

 ▬ A **semibreve rest** can also be used to indicate a whole bar's rest in any time signature.

crescendo – tells you to get gradually louder.

59 Feed the birds

Richard M Sherman and Robert B Sherman

58 Jupiter (teacher's part)

step 14

staccato – the dot tells you to make the note short and detached.

cresc. indicates a long crescendo. It tells you to get gradually louder until you reach the next dynamic mark.

Con spirito – with spirit.

Start ***Kalinka*** slowly and get gradually faster.

60 Kalinka

28-29

traditional Russian

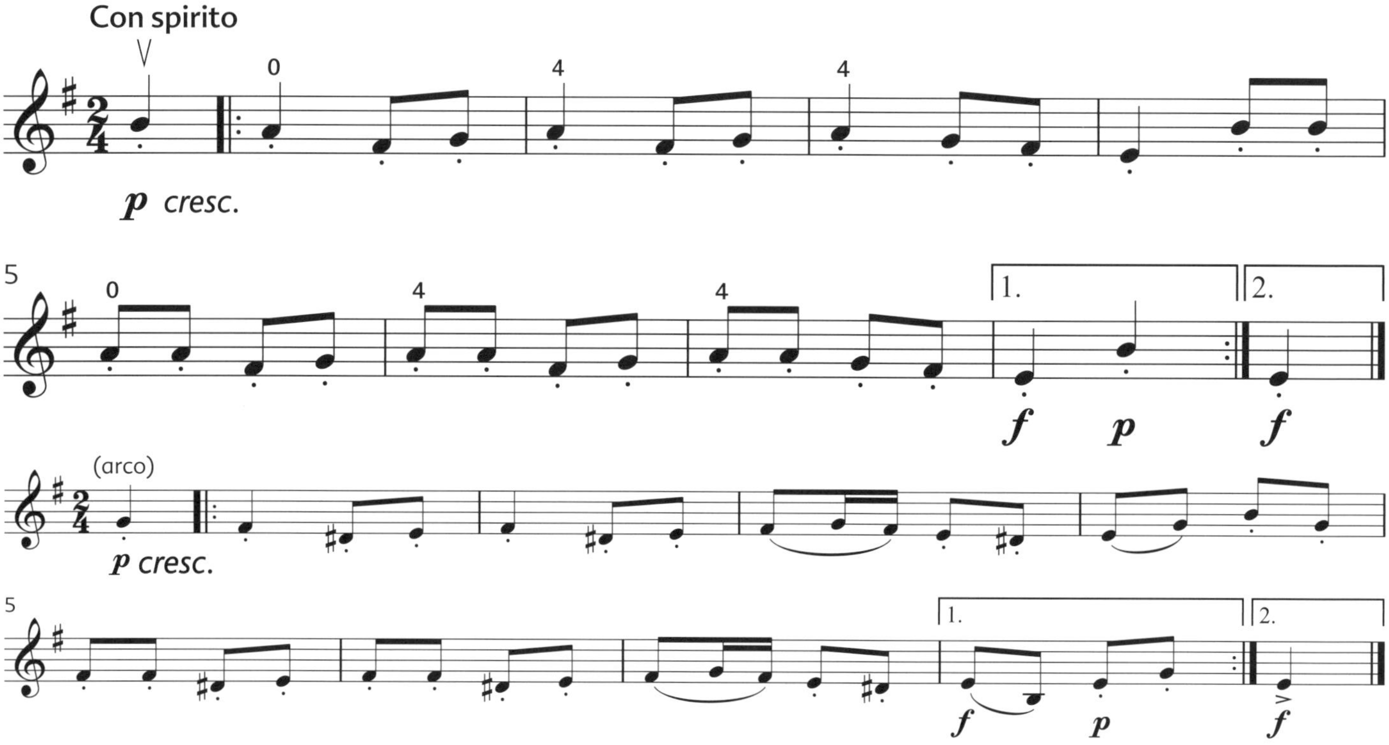

61 The old bazaar in Cairo

30-31

traditional

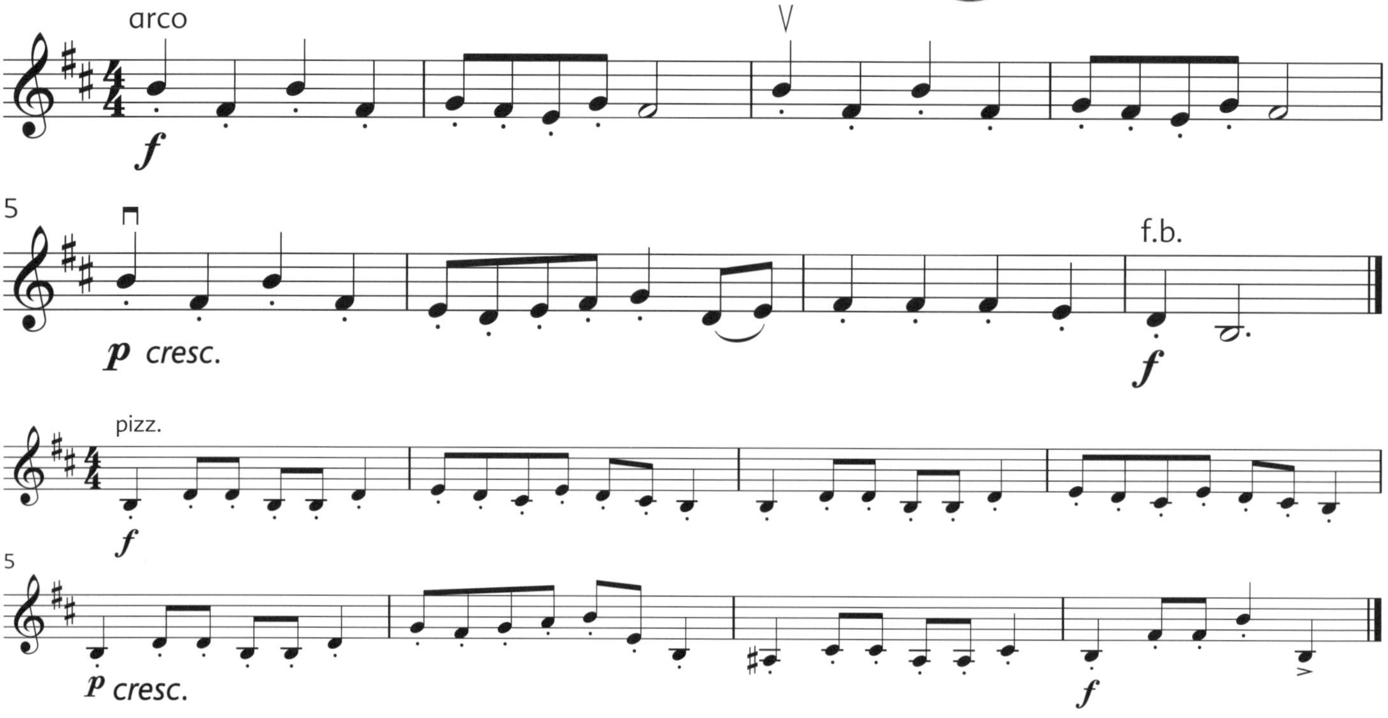

 To practise staccato notes, play your teacher's part in

no. 1 *Pizz on D*
no. 5 *Supercalifragilisticexpialidocious*

mp (mezzo piano) tells you to play moderately quietly.

mf (mezzo forte) tells you to play moderately loudly.

A **tenuto** line tells you to hold the note for its full length.

quaver rest – lasts for half a crotchet beat of silence.

62 Muck! (round)

traditional

Waltz

Oh you can't put your muck in our dust-bin, our dust-bin, our dust-bin, you can't put your muck in our dust-bin, our dust-bin's full.

Fish 'n' chips and vin-e-gar, pep-per pep-per pep-per pot. At-choo!

Fish 'n' chips and vin-e-gar, pep-per pep-per pep-per pot.

One cup of tea, two cup of tea, three cup of tea, four cup of tea,

five cup of tea, six cup of tea, sev'n cup of tea, eight.

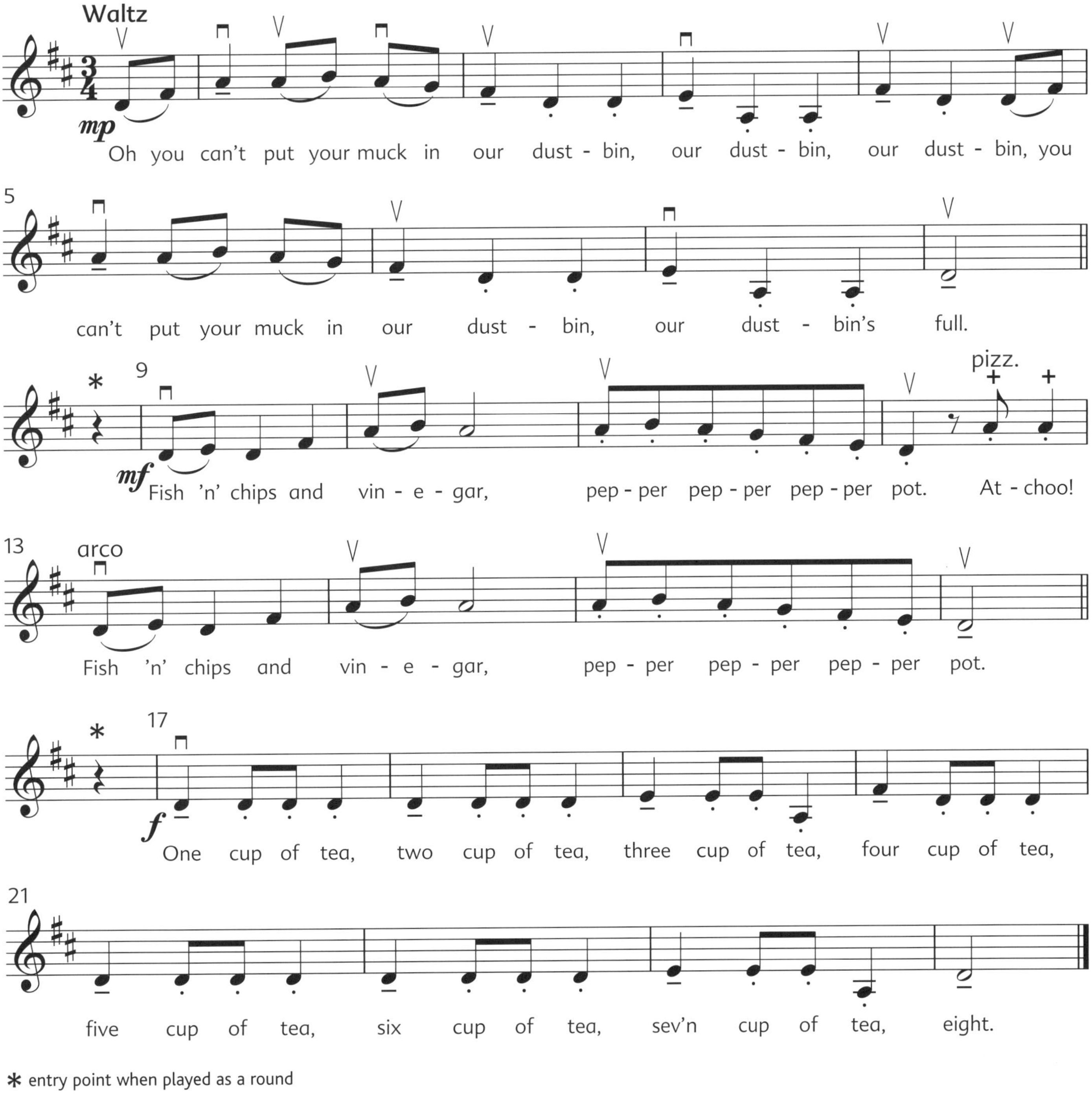

* entry point when played as a round

 These are **non-legato ties**. They tell you to play both notes in the same bow, but to make them slightly detached by stopping the bow for a moment in mid-stroke.

This technique is sometimes called **hooked bowing**.

diminuendo – tells you to get gradually quieter.

63 Waltz

Franz Lehar

Moderato – at a moderate speed.

64 Puff the magic dragon (duet)

36-37

Peter Yarrow and Leonard Upton

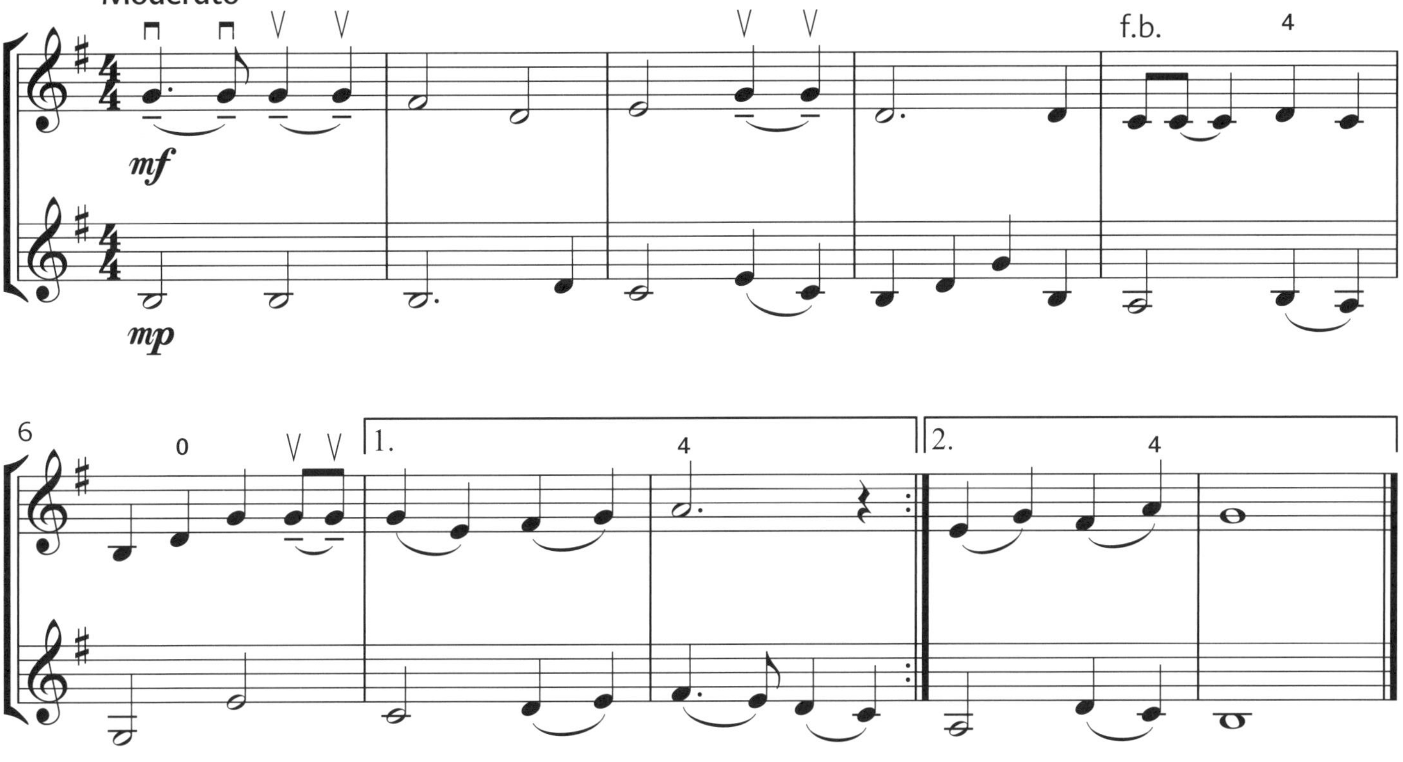

Moderato
mf
mp
f.b.
4
6
0
1.
2.

65 Dumplins

38-39

traditional Caribbean

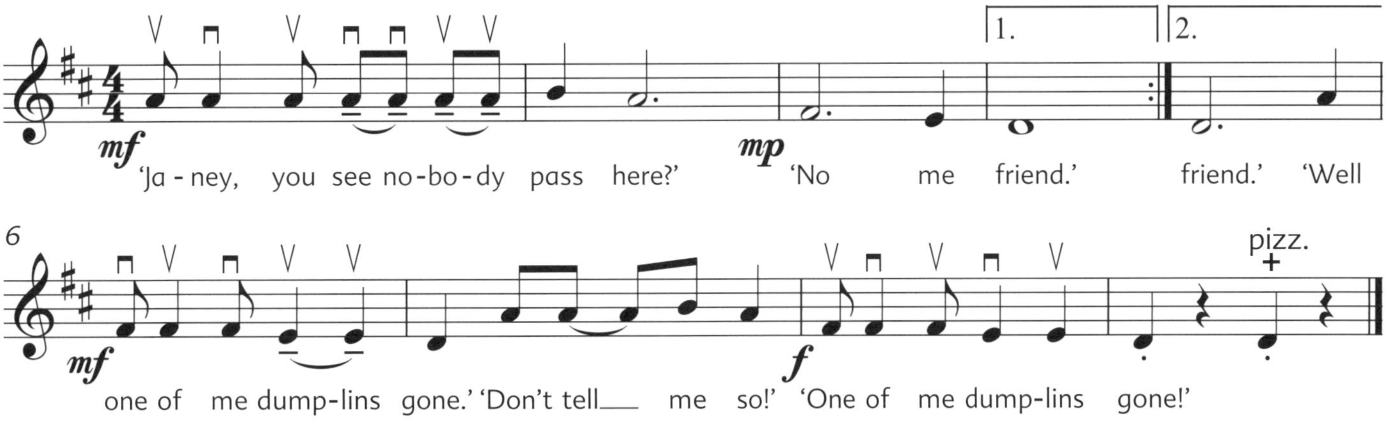

1.
2.
mf
'Ja - ney, you see no-bo-dy pass here?'
mp
'No me friend.' friend.' 'Well
6
mf
one of me dump-lins gone.' 'Don't tell___ me so!' 'One of me dump-lins gone!'
f
pizz.

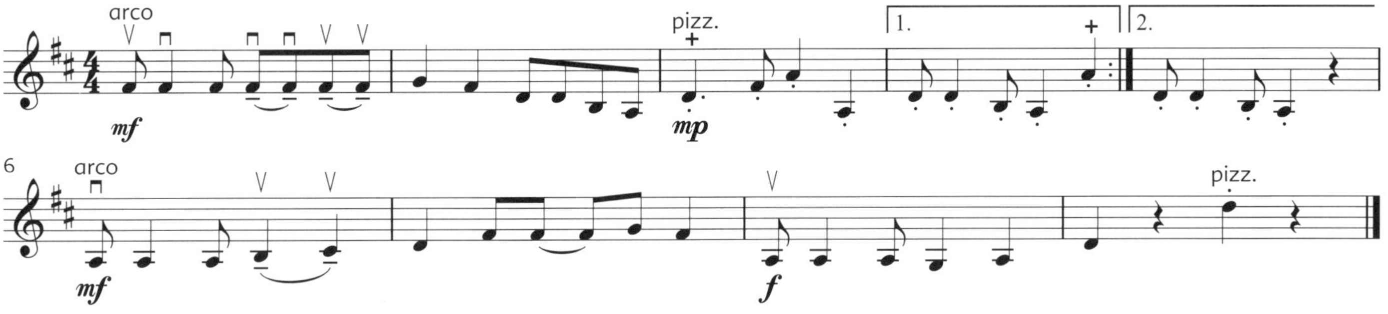

arco
mf
pizz.
mp
1.
2.
6
arco
mf
f
pizz.

step 15

 **6/8** time signature – means there are six quaver beats to the bar.

Count six quavers: or two dotted crotchets:

Try playing these rhythms on any open string:

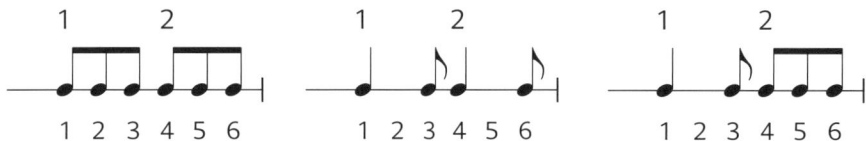

66 Row, row, row your boat (round)    traditional

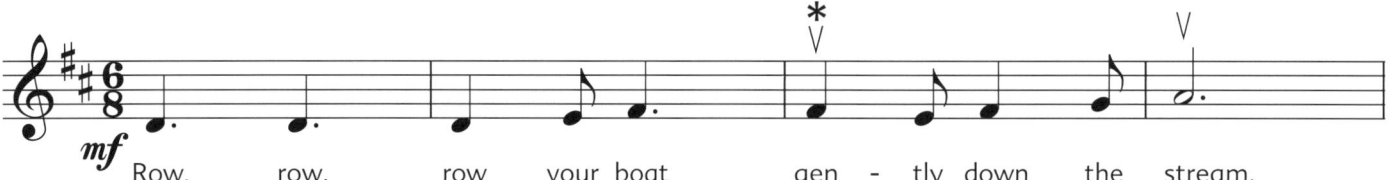

* entry point when played as a round

67 Pop! goes the weasel    traditional

Ostinato accompaniment (play four times)

Compose your own ostinato accompaniment to go with *Row, row, row your boat* or *Pop! goes the weasel*.

Play the open strings D and A and use any of the $\frac{6}{8}$ rhythms opposite.

68 Dance of the cuckoos (duet)

Marvin Hatley

69 The shepherdess (round)

traditional French

✳ entry point when played as a round

D major arpeggio

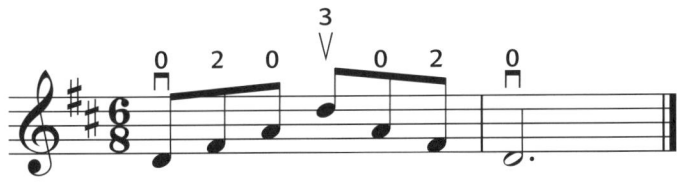

G major arpeggio

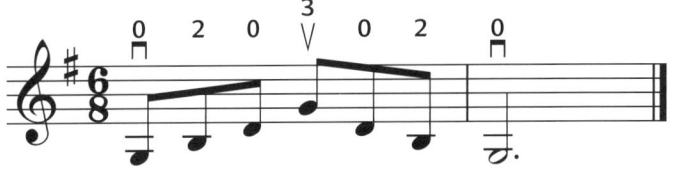

70 We're off to see the Wizard

48-49

words E Y Harburg, music Harold Arlen

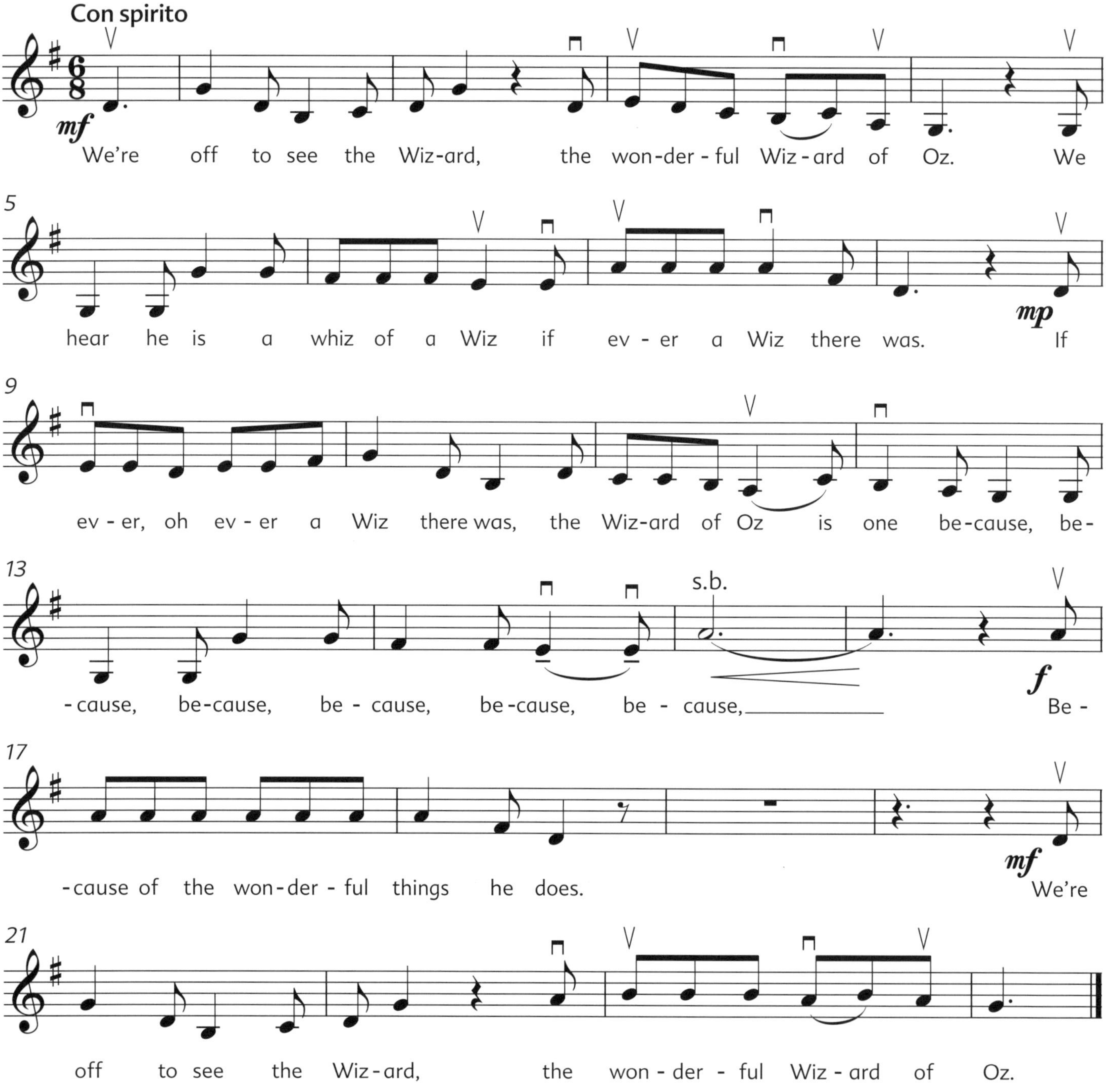
Con spirito
mf
We're off to see the Wiz-ard, the won-der-ful Wiz-ard of Oz. We
5
hear he is a whiz of a Wiz if ev - er a Wiz there was.
mp
If
9
ev - er, oh ev - er a Wiz there was, the Wiz-ard of Oz is one be-cause, be-
13
s.b.
-cause, be-cause, be - cause, be-cause, be - cause,
f
Be -
17
-cause of the won-der - ful things he does.
mf
We're
21
off to see the Wiz-ard, the won - der - ful Wiz - ard of Oz.

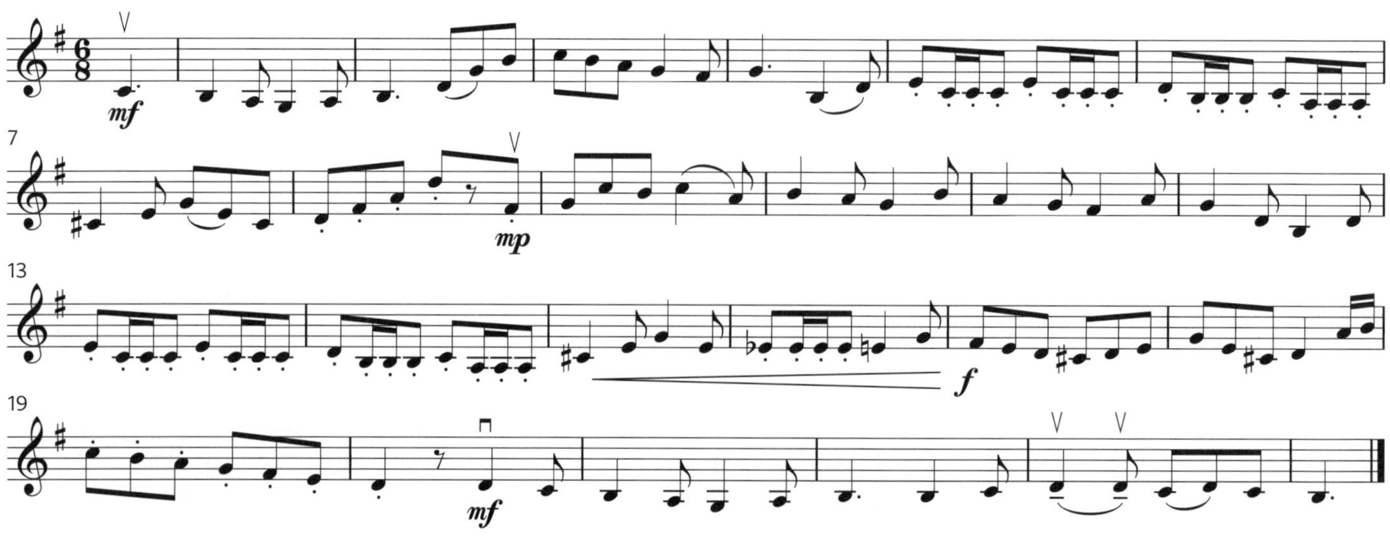
mf
7
mp
13
f
19
mf

step 16

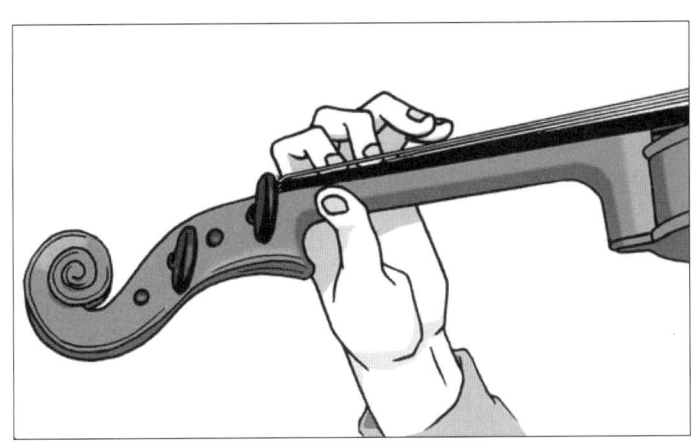

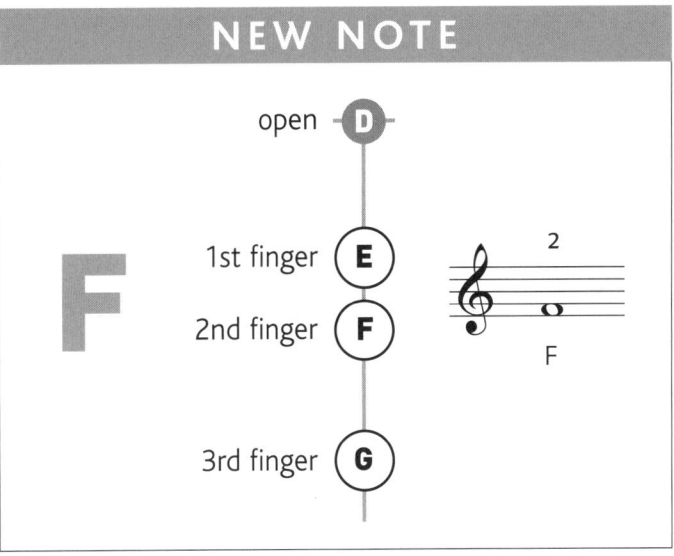

 F is halfway between E and F♯ – a semitone higher than E and a semitone lower than F♯.

Misterioso – mysteriously.

Try playing *Egyptian snake dance* pizzicato. Then play it arco, but make each note staccato (leaving out the slurs and ties).

71 Egyptian snake dance

traditional

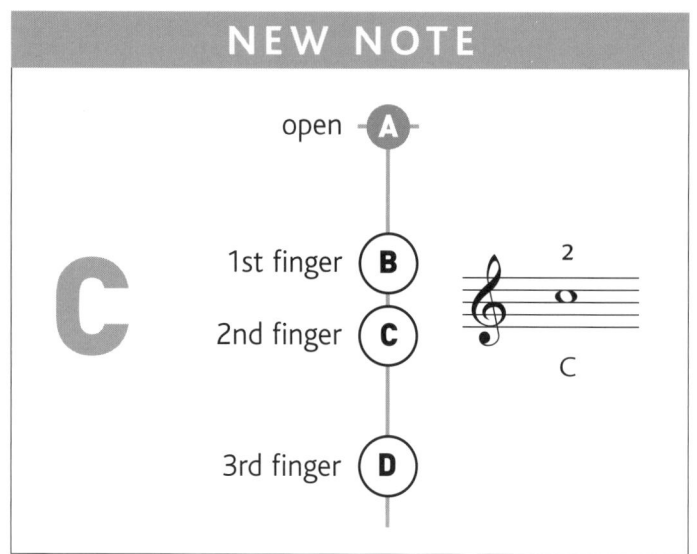

72 Shalom (round)

traditional Israeli

Sha - lom, cha - ve - rim, sha - lom, cha - ve - rim, sha - lom, sha - lom. Le -
-hi - tra - ot, le - hi - tra - ot, sha - lom, sha - lom.

✱ entry point when played as a round

73 Summer is icumen in (round)

traditional

✱ entry point when played as a round

74 Part of your world (duet)

56–57

words Howard Ashman,
music Alan Menken

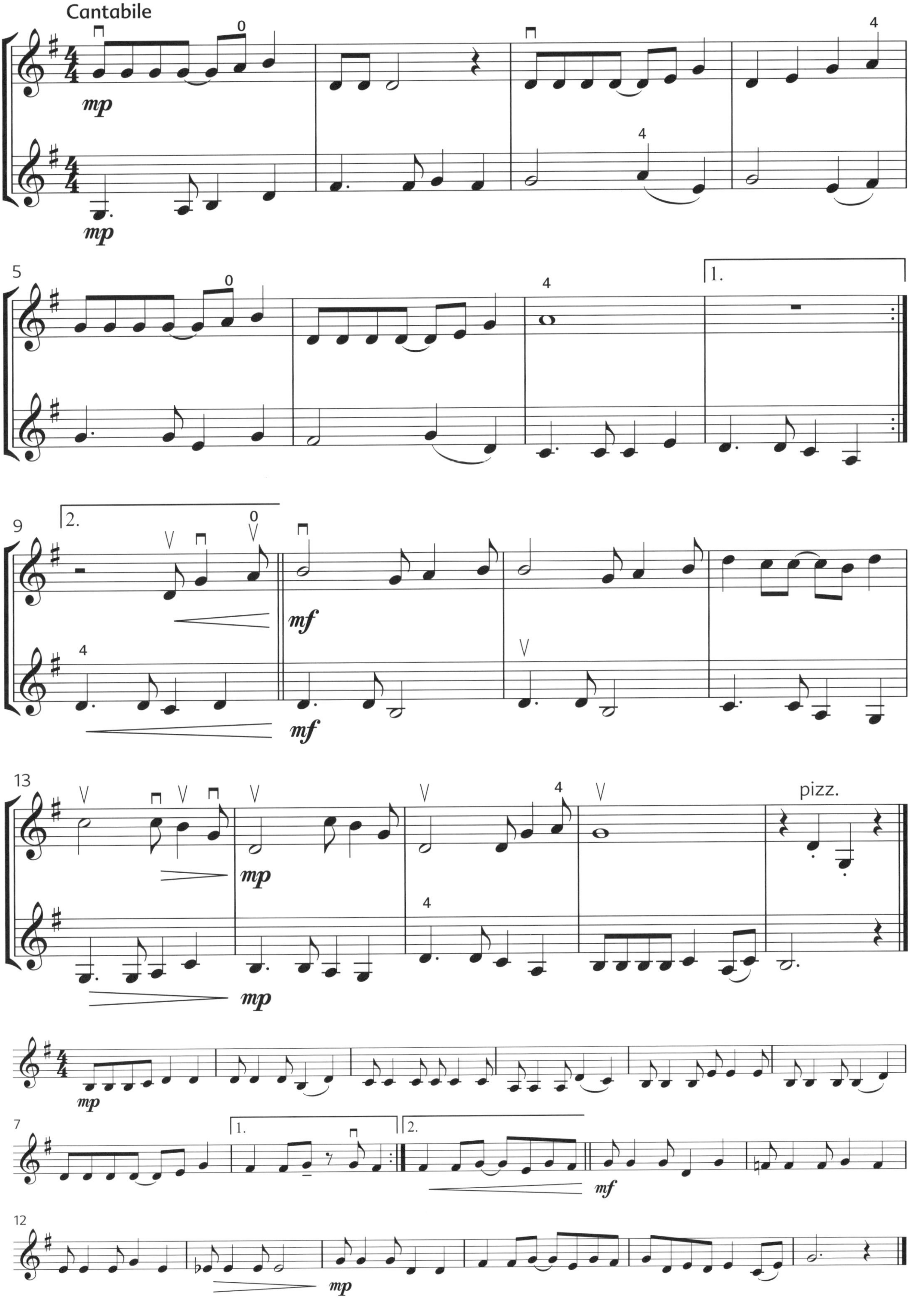

step 17

 ♬ **semiquaver** – worth a quarter of a crotchet beat.

Semiquavers can be grouped like this:

Look carefully at the key signature before you start each piece, so that you can decide where to place your second finger.

Look at the accompaniments for *Short'nin' bread* and *What shall we do with the drunken sailor*? Check their key signatures. What do you notice? Where will you place your second finger?

75 Short'nin' bread (duet)

Jacques Wolfe and Clement Wood

76 What shall we do with the drunken sailor? (duet)

traditional

 To practise semiquavers, play your teacher's part in no. 8 *Mobile phone*.

77 Winter wonderland

62-63

words Richard Smith, music Felix Bernard

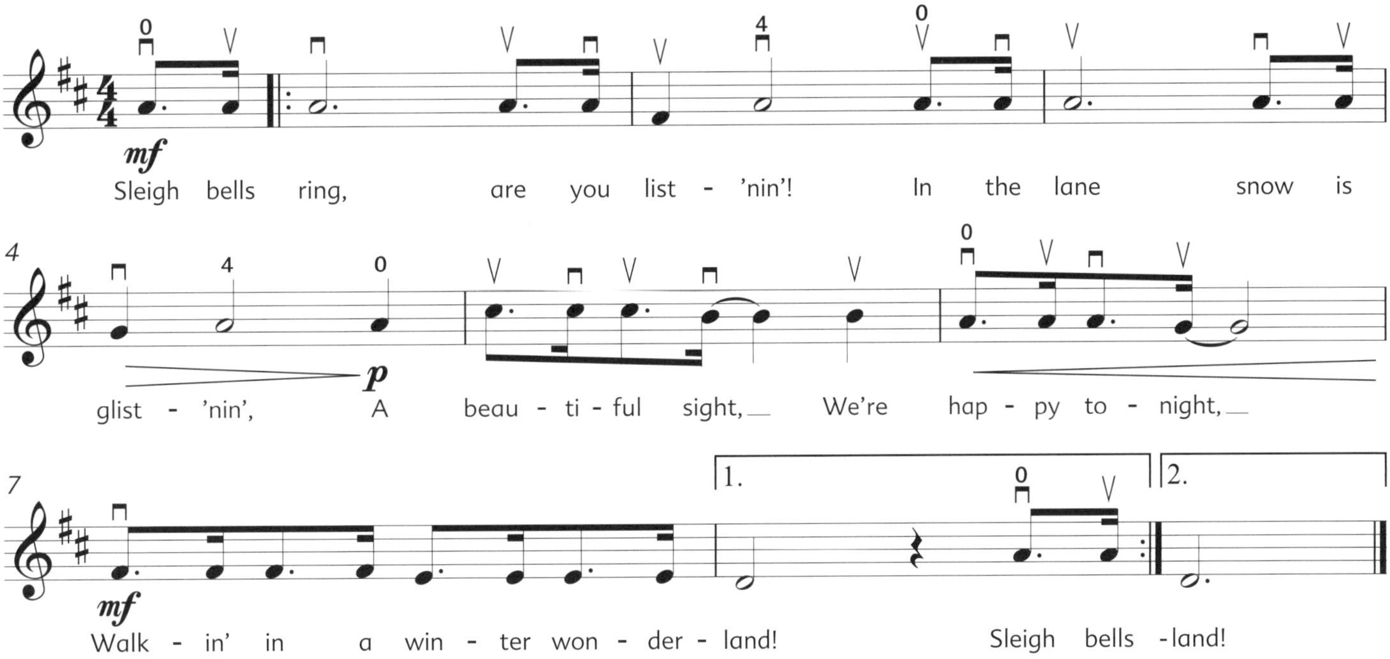
Sleigh bells ring, are you list - 'nin'! In the lane snow is
glist - 'nin', A beau - ti - ful sight, We're hap - py to - night,
Walk - in' in a win - ter won - der - land! Sleigh bells -land!

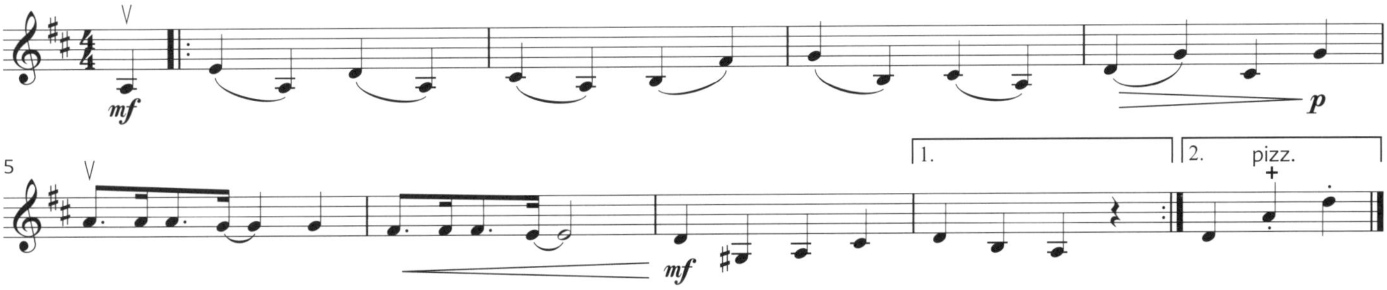
pizz.

78 EastEnders

64-65

Leslie Osborne and Simon May

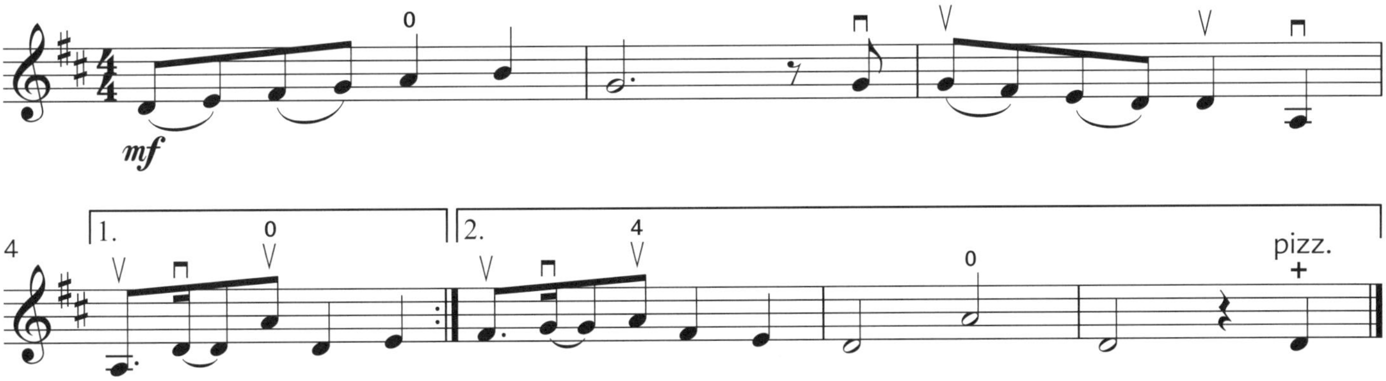
pizz.

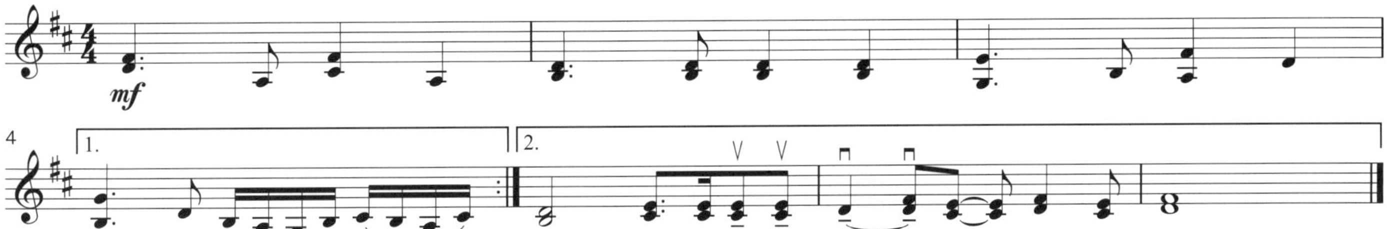

step 18

★ All the tunes in this step use a mixture of both positions of the 2nd finger.

⌒ **pause** – tells you to hold a note for longer than its written value.

79 Happy birthday (duet)

Patty S Hill and Mildred Hill

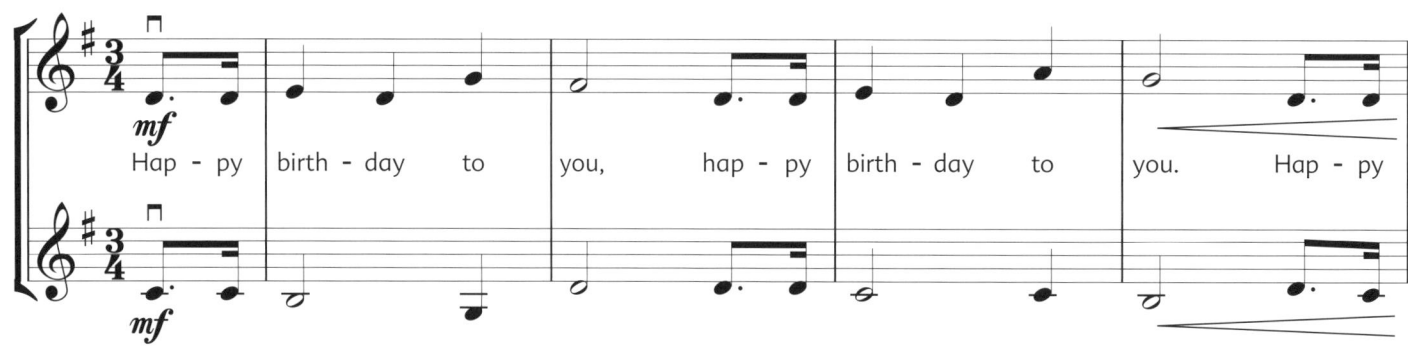

Hap - py birth - day to you, hap - py birth - day to you. Hap - py

birth - day dear Mis - sak, hap - py birth - day to you.

80 Heigh-ho

words Larry Morey, music Frank Churchill

'Heigh - ho', 'Heigh - ho', To make your trou - bles go, Just keep on sing - ing

all day long 'Heigh - ho', 'Heigh - ho', 'Heigh - ho', 'Heigh - ho', 'Heigh - ho'.

 The next three tunes use both positions of the 2nd finger on the D string: F♯ and F.

Try playing **The Addams family** pizzicato to make it sound even spookier. Then ask your teacher to play the tune, while you do the finger clicks.

81 The Addams family (duet)

Vic Mizzy

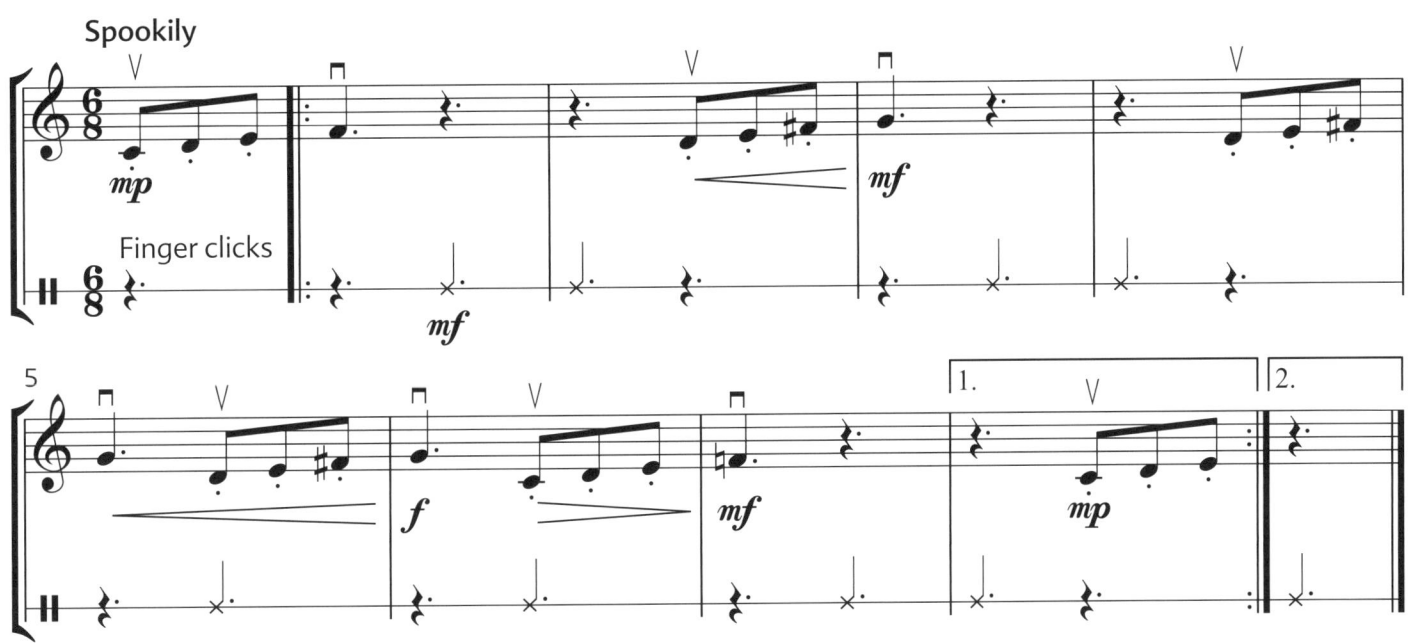

82 The mocking bird

traditional Caribbean

83 Chim chim cher-ee

Richard M Sherman and Robert B Sherman

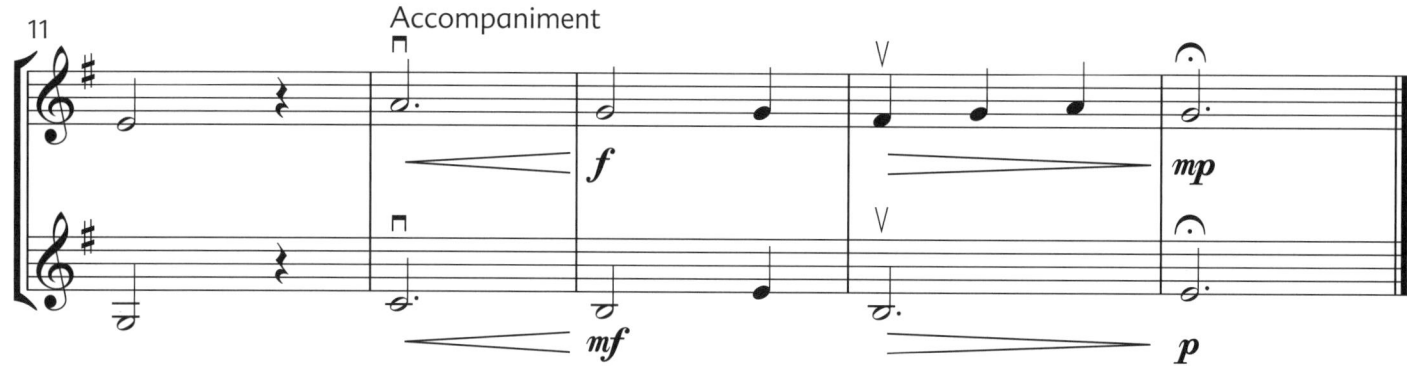
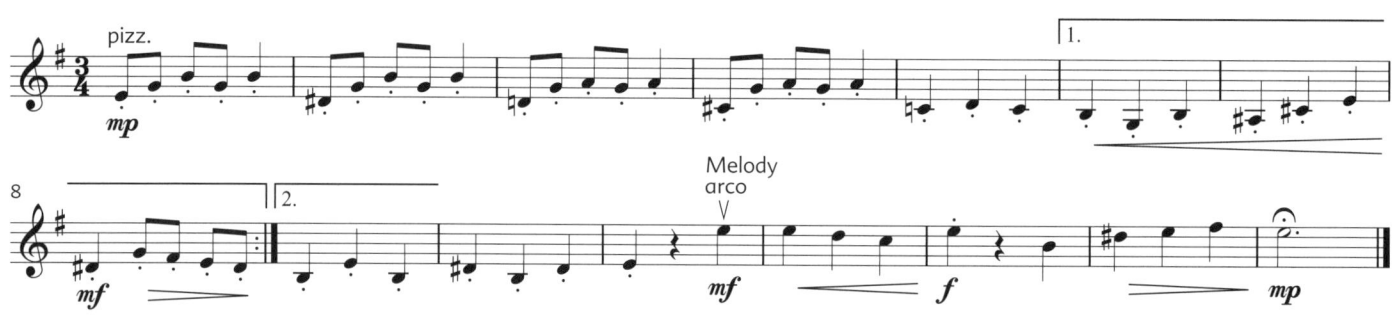

 To practise both positions of the 2nd finger, play your teacher's part in

no. 22 **Road monsters**

no. 3 **Bobby Shafto**

step 19

NEW NOTES

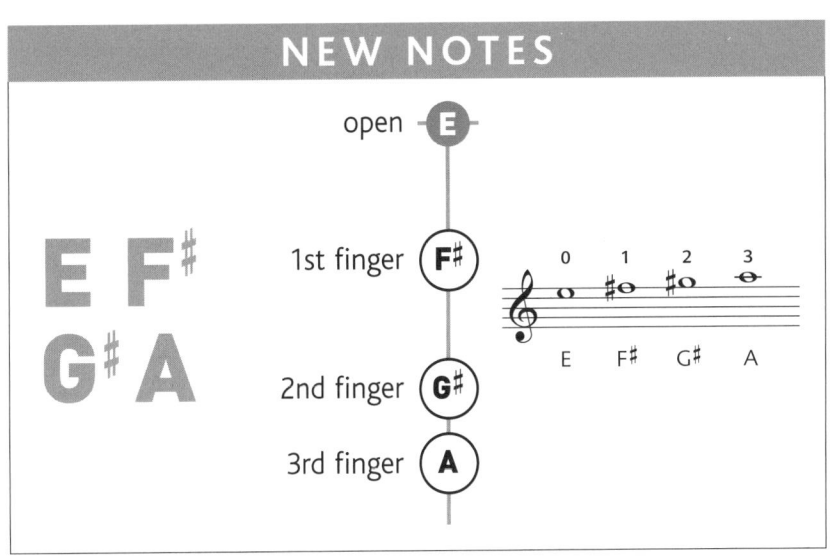

84 Ragamuffin's rag

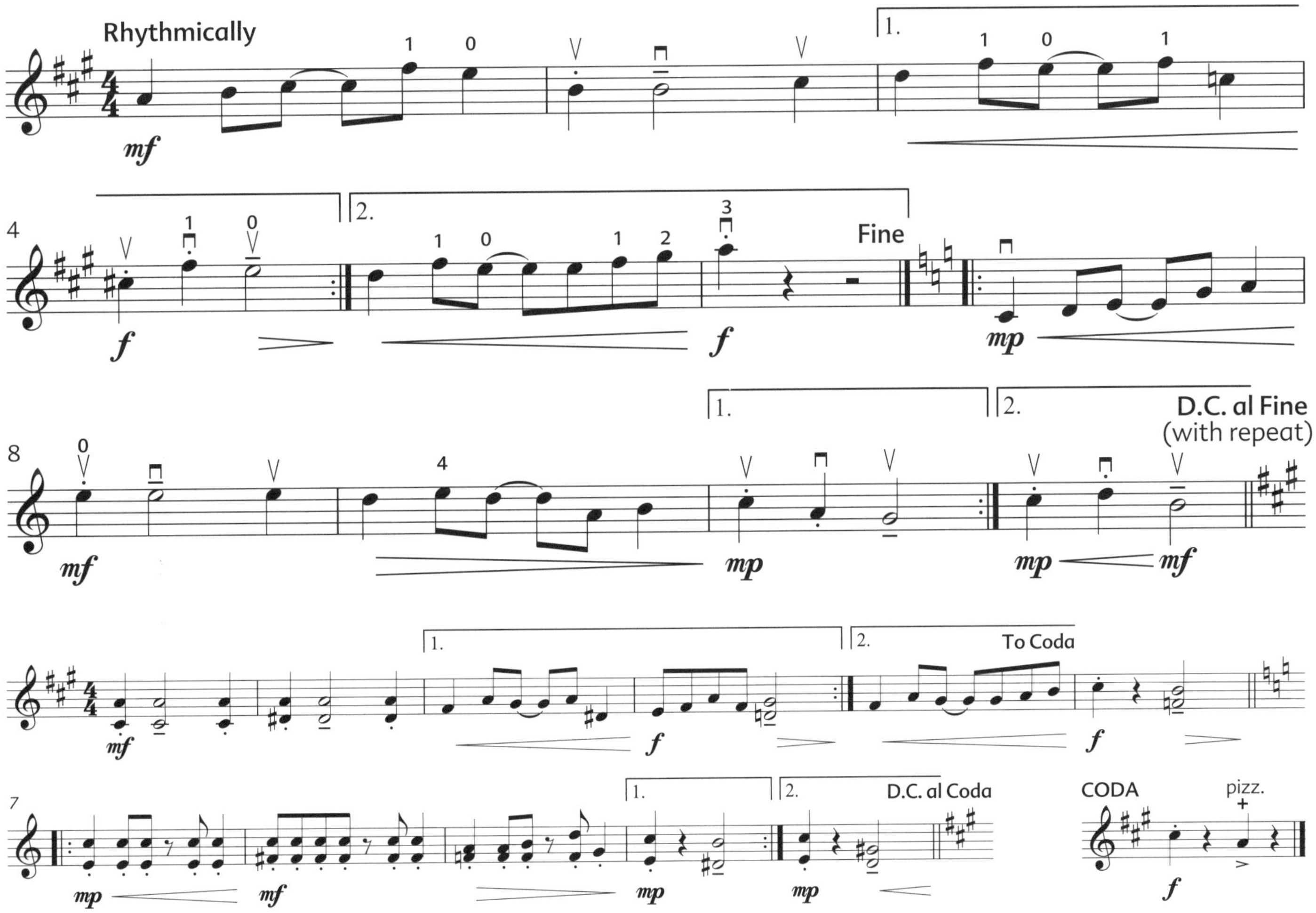

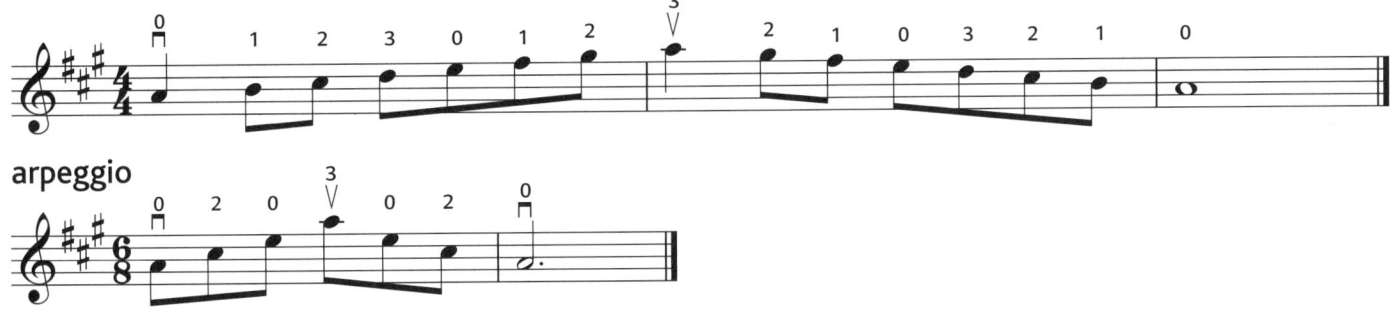

A major

scale

The finger pattern is the same as that of D major, starting on the A string.

arpeggio

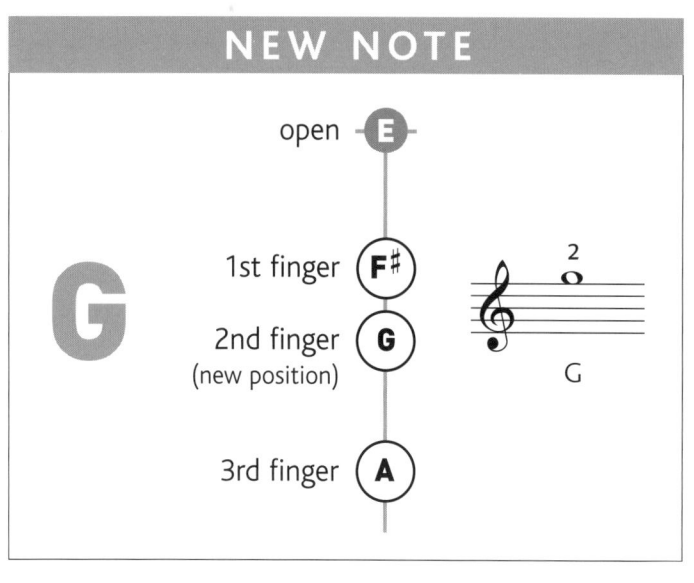

85 Who will buy? 78-79

Lionel Bart

Who will buy this won-der-ful morn-ing? Such a sky you nev-er did see!

Who will tie it up with a rib-bon, And put it in a box for me?

G major
scale (two octaves)

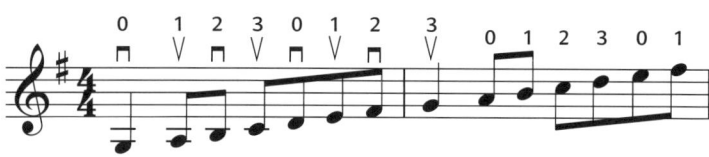

arpeggio (two octaves)

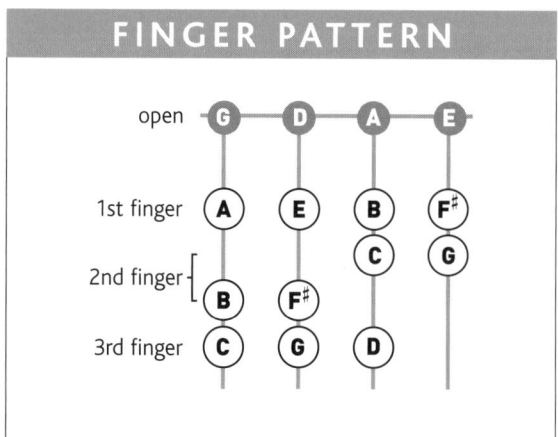

86 Beauty and the Beast (duet)

80–81

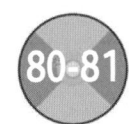

words Howard Ashman, music Alan Menken

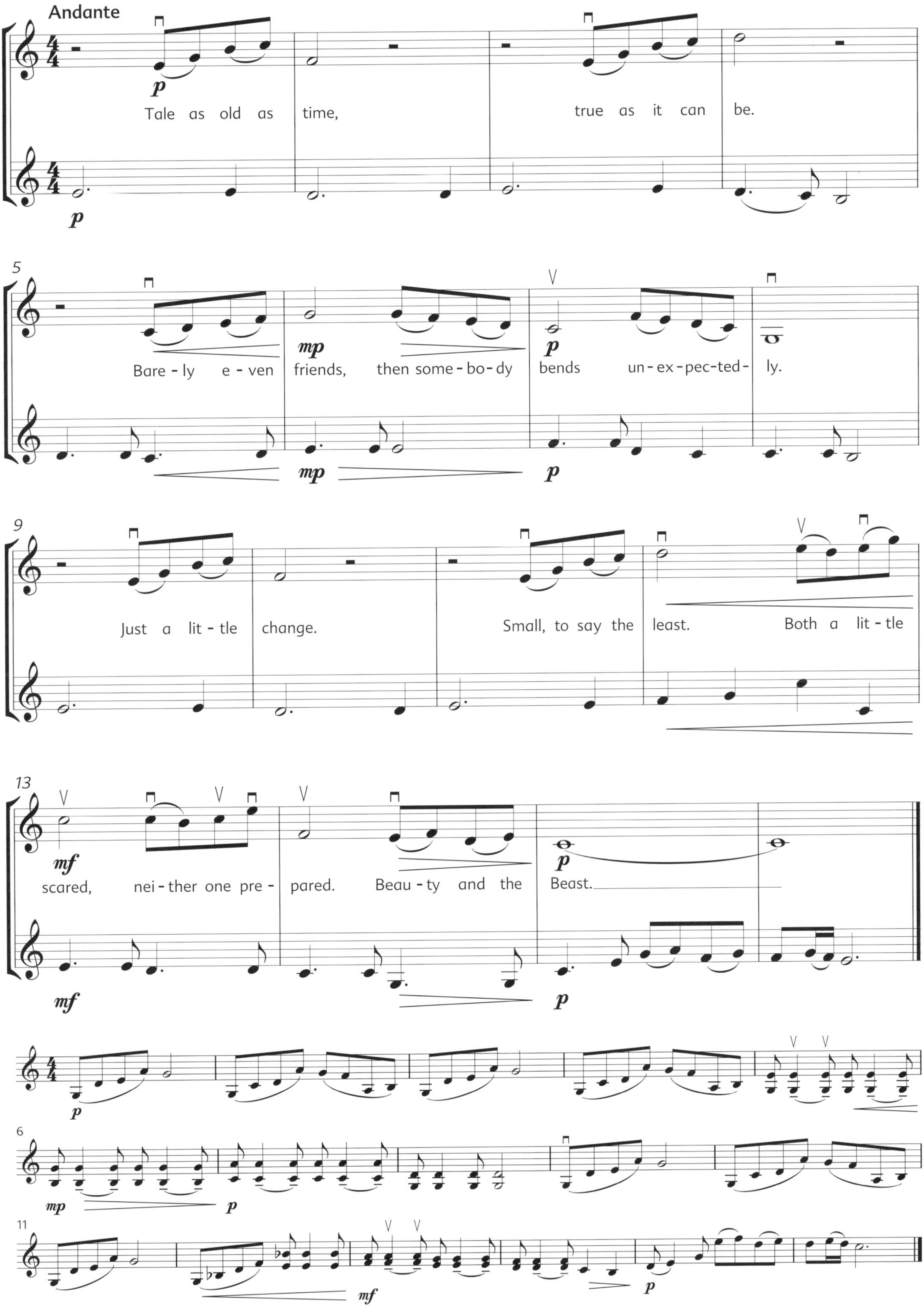
Andante
Tale as old as time, true as it can be.
Bare - ly e - ven friends, then some - bo - dy bends un - ex - pec - ted - ly.
Just a lit - tle change. Small, to say the least. Both a lit - tle
scared, nei - ther one pre - pared. Beau - ty and the Beast.

step 20

 *Barcarolle* contains three-note slurs.
Play each slurred group of notes in one bow.

87 Barcarolle (duet)

Jacques Offenbach

 rall. tells you to get gradually slower. It is short for **rallentando**.
Nocturne contains four-note slurs. Play all four notes in one bow.

88 Nocturne

Aleksander Borodin

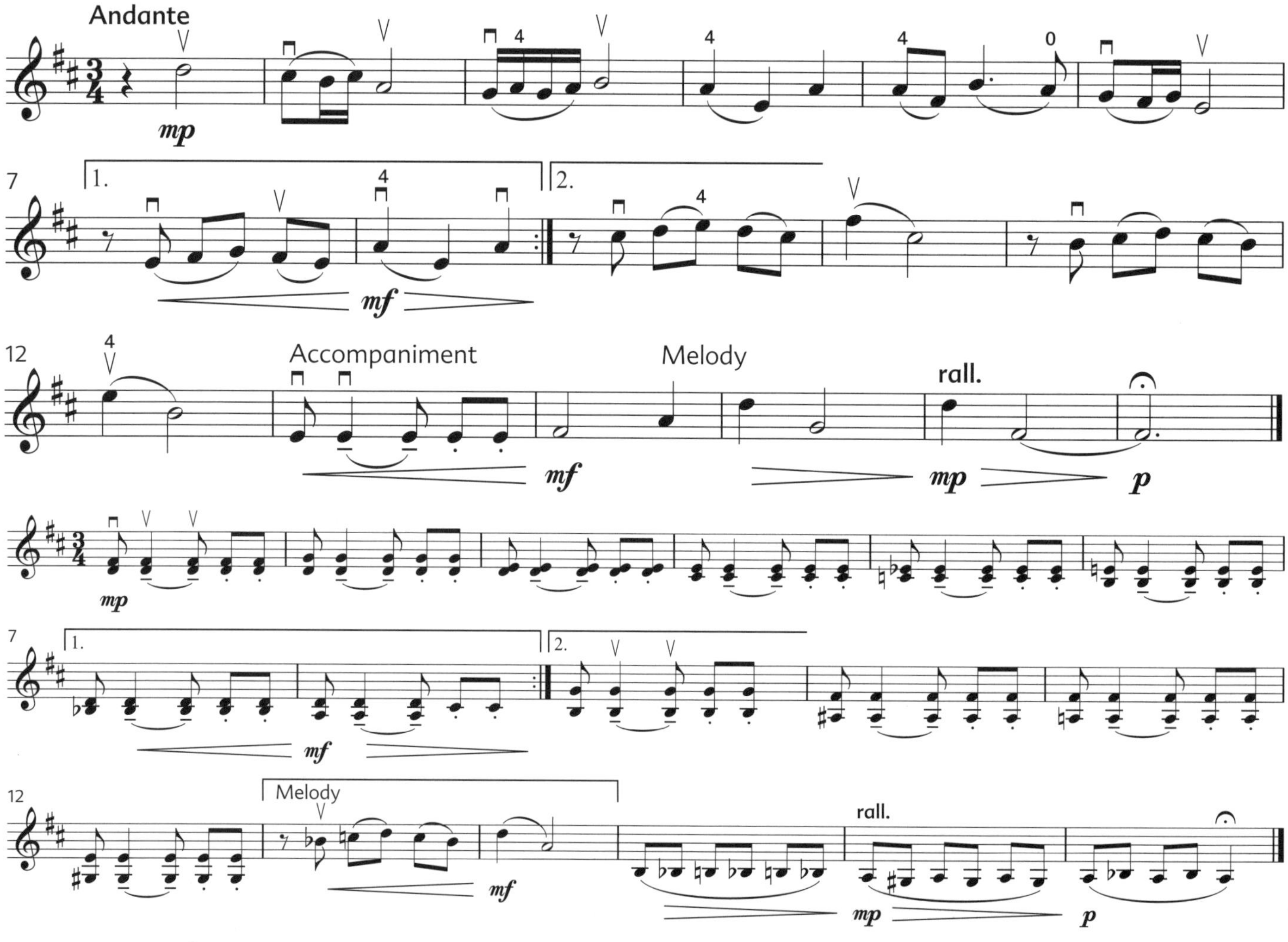

Acknowledgements

The author and publisher would like to thank the following for their help in the preparation of this book: Jeremy Birchall, Patricia Birchall, Jennifer Boston, Adrian Bradbury, Emily Brayshaw, Chris Bryant, Helen Crayford, Janet Crew, Louise Dearsley, Tanya Demidova, Philip Dukes, Heather Fleck, David W Giles, Emily Haward, Jocelyn Lucus, Andrew Lynwood, Grace Lynwood, Barry Newland, Malcolm Pallant, Maja Passchier, Aoife Patarot-Hinds, Roland Roberts, Sheena Roberts, Valérie Saint-Pierre, Elaine Scott, Michelle Simpson, Holly Stirling, Dominic Viall, Matthew Watson and Allison Whitehead. Very special thanks go to Carla Moss.

We are grateful to the following copyright owners who have kindly granted permission for the reprinting of these items:

Beauty and the Beast (from Beauty and the Beast) Words by Howard Ashman, Music by Alan Menken, © 1991 Wonderland Music Company Inc and Walt Disney Music Co Ltd, USA. Warner/Chappell Artemis Music Ltd, London W6 8BS. Reproduced by permission of Faber Music Ltd. All Rights Reserved;

Chim chim cher-ee (From Mary Poppins) Words and Music by Richard M Sherman and Robert B Sherman © 1963 Wonderland Music Company Inc, Warner/Chappell Artemis Music Ltd, London W6 8BS. Reproduced by permission of Faber Music Ltd. All Rights Reserved;

Dance of the cuckoos (Ku-ku) By T Marvin Hatley © 1930, 1932 Hatley Music Company, USA. Robert Kingston Music Limited, 8/9 Frith Street, London W1. Used by permission of Music Sales Ltd. All Rights Reserved. International Copyright Secured;

Eastenders by Leslie Osborne & Simon May © 1985 ATV Music. Sony/ATV Music Publishing (UK) Limited, 10 Great Marlborough Street, London W1. Used by permission of Music Sales Ltd. All Rights Reserved. International Copyright Secured;

Edelweiss from the Sound of Music. Words by Oscar Hammerstein II, music by Richard Rodgers © 1959 by Richard Rodgers and Oscar Hammerstein II. Copyright renewed. This arrangement © 2002 by Williamson Music. Williamson Music owner of publication and allied rights throughout the world. International Copyright Secured. All Rights Reserved;

Feed the birds (from Mary Poppins) Music and Words by Richard M Sherman and Robert B Sherman © 1964 Wonderland Music Company Inc, Warner/Chappell Artemis Music Ltd, London W6 8BS. Reproduced by permission of Faber Music Ltd. All Rights Reserved;

Halfway down the stairs Text by A.A. Milne and Music by H. Fraser Simson. Copyright under the Berne Convention;

Happy birthday to you Words and Music by Patty S Hill and Mildred Hill © 1935 (renewed 1962) Summy Birchard Inc. Keith Prowse Music Publishing Co Ltd. Reproduced by International Music Publications (a trading name of Faber Music Ltd). All Rights Reserved;

Heigh ho Words by Larry Morey. Music by Frank Churchill © copyright 1938 by Bourne Co. Copyright Renewed. This arrangement © copyright 2002 by Bourne Co. All Rights Reserved. International Copyright Secured. Printed with permission from Bourne Music Ltd;

Lieutenant Kijé (Troika), op. 60 by Prokofieff. Copyright © 1936 by Hawkes & Son (London) Ltd. Reproduced by permission of Boosey & Hawkes Music Publishers Ltd;

(Meet) The Flintstones Words and Music by Joseph Barbera, William Hanna and Hoyt Curtin © 1960 Warner/Tamerlane Publishing Corp, USA. Warner/Chappell North America Ltd, Londond W6 8BS. Reproduced by permission of Faber Music Ltd. All Rights Reserved;

Morningtown ride © 1959 by Amadeo Brio Music Inc. Administered by MCS Music Ltd, 32 Lexington Street, London W1F OLQ;

Off to France in the morning, One finger dance, Spinning wheel, Summer shine and **Windmill song** © 1985 Peter Davey;

Part of your world (from The Little Mermaid) Music by Alan Menken, Words by Howard Ashman © 1988 Walt Disney Music (USA) Co Ltd and Wonderland Music Company Inc, USA. Warner/Chappell Artemis Music Ltd, London W6 8BS. Reproduced by permission of Faber Music Ltd. All Rights Reserved;

Puff the magic dragon Words and Music by Leonard Lipton and Peter Yarrow. Copyright © 1963 Pepamar Music Corp and Honalee Melodies, USA (70%) Warner/Chappell North America Ltd. 30% Cherry Lane Music Publishing Inc. Reproduced by permission of Faber Music Ltd. All Rights Reserved;

Short'nin' bread © Copyright 1928 (renewed) by Harold Flammer Music (ASCAP), a division of Shawnee Press Inc. International Copyright Secured. All Rights Reserved. Reproduced by permission of Chester Music Limited;

Stand by me Words and music by Ben E King, Jerry Leiber and Mike Stoller © 1961 (renewed) Jerry Leiber Music, Mike Stoller Music and Trio Music Company INC. This arrangement © 2002 Jerry Leiber Music, Mike Stoller Music and Trio Music Company INC. All Rights Reserved;

Supercalifragilisticexpialidocious (From Mary Poppins) Words and Music by Richard M Sherman and Robert B Sherman © 1964 Wonderland Music Company Inc, Warner/Chappell Artemis Music Ltd, London W6 8BS. Reproduced by permission of Faber Music Ltd. All Rights Reserved;

Tea for two Words by Irving Caesar, music by Vincent Youmans © 1924 Harms Inc, USA (50%) Chappell Music Ltd and (50%) Warner/Chappell Music Ltd, London W6 8BS. Reproduced by permission of Faber Music Ltd. All Rights Reserved;

The Addams family Words and Music by Vic Mizzy © 1963 Unison Music Publishing Co Ltd. EMI Music Publishing Ltd. Reproduced by permission of International Music Publications Ltd (a trading name of Faber Music Ltd). All Rights Reserved;

The hippopotamus song Words by Michael Flanders, Music by Donald Swann © 1952 Chappell Music Ltd, London W6 8BS. Reproduced by permission of Faber Music Ltd. All Rights Reserved;

The way you look tonight Words by Dorothy Fields, Music by Jerome Kern © 1936 T B Harms Company and Aldi Music, USA (50%) Shapiro Bernstein & Co Limited, New York NY 10022-5718, USA. Reproduced by permission of Faber Music Ltd. All Rights Reserved;

Theme from Jupiter from **The Planets, op. 32** Music by Gustav Holst © copyright 1921 Goodwin & Tabb Limited. Transferred to J Curwen & Sons Limited, 8/9 Frith Street, London W1D 3JB. All Rights Reserved. Reproduced by permission;

Waltz from **The Merry Widow** Music by Franz Lehar. © 1928 Ludwig KG Doblinger Musik-Verlag. Chappell Music Ltd. Reproduced by permission of Faber Music Ltd. All Rights Reserved;

We All Stand Together Words and Music by Paul McCartney © 1984 MPL Communications Ltd. All Rights Reserved, Used By Permission;

We're off to see the wizard Words by E Y Harburg, music by Harold Arlen © 1939 EMI Catalogue Partnership, EMI Feist Catalog Inc and EMI United Partnership Ltd, USA. Worldwide print rights controlled by Warner Bros. Reproduced by permission of Faber Music Ltd. All Rights Reserved;

Whistle while you work Words by Larry Morey. Music by Frank Churchill. © copyright 1937 by Bourne Co. All Rights Reserved. International Copyright Secured. Printed with permission from Bourne Music Ltd;

Who will buy? © 1960 Lakeview Music Publishing Co Ltd. Suite 2.07, Plaza 535 Kings Road, London SW10 0SZ. International Copyright Secured. All Rights Reserved. Used by permission;

Winter wonderland Words by Dick Smith, Music by Felix Bernard © 1934 Francis Day & Hunter Ltd (For Europe excl. France, Belgium, Monaco, Italy, Spain, Portugal, Holland & French-speaking part of Switzerland) and Warner/Chappell North America ltd (For France, Belgium, Monaco, Italy, Spain, Portugal, Holland & French-speaking part of Switzerland). Reproduced by permission of International Music Publications Ltd (a trading name of Faber Music Ltd) and Faber Music Limited. All Rights Reserved.

All other original pieces and arrangements are copyright A&C Black. Every effort has been made to trace and acknowledge copyright owners. If any right has been omitted, the publishers offer their apologies and will rectify this in subsequent editions following notification.

Recording

Violin played by Roland Roberts
Piano played by Helen Crayford
Engineered by Matthew Moore and Andrew Lynwood
All other arrangements by Barry Gibson (5, 22, 43, 60, 84)
and David Moses (10, 31, 58, 70, 88)

All rights reserved. Copying, public performance and broadcasting – in whole or in part – of the recording are prohibited by law.

Third edition 2009
Reprinted 2009, 2013
A&C Black Publishers Ltd, an imprint of
Bloomsbury Publishing Plc
50 Bedford Square, London, WC1B 3DP
© Copyright 2009, 1988 A&C Black Publishers Ltd
Pupil's book ISBN 978-1-4081-1460-5
Pupil's book + 2 CDs ISBN 978-1-4081-1461-2

Technical diagrams by Kanako Damerum and Yuzuru Takasaki
Cover illustration by Q2AMedia
Design by Jane Tetzlaff and Tatiana Demidova
Music setting by Christopher Hussey and Jeanne Fisher
Edited by Chris Barstow, Christopher Hussey and Jane Sebba

Photocopying prohibited

All rights reserved. No part of this publication may be reproduced in any form or by any means – photographic, electronic or mechanical, including photocopying, recording, taping or information storage and retrieval systems – without the prior permission in writing of the publishers.

This book is produced using paper that is made from wood grown in managed, sustainable forests. It is natural, renewable and recyclable. The logging and manufacturing processes conform to the environmental regulations of the country of origin.

Printed by Caligraving Ltd, Thetford, Norfolk

INDEX

A friend in DEED	10
A stitch in time	14
A tisket, a tasket	6
Au clair de la lune	23
Barcarolle (duet)	87
Beauty and the Beast (duet)	86
Big Ben (duet)	34
Bobby Shafto	3
Brown bread (duet)	33
Call of the carousel	48
Chim chim cher-ee	83
Clown dance	21
Dance of the cuckoos (duet)	68
Daydreamer	45
Dumplins	65
EastEnders	78
Edelweiss	50
Eee-abba-dabba-dee!	12
Egyptian snake dance	71
Feed the birds	59
Fiddle fanfare (duet/trio)	9
Frère Jacques	15
Halfway down the stairs	31
Happy birthday (duet)	79
Heigh-ho	80
Hot cross buns (duet)	18
I came from Alabama	42
Jupiter	58
Kalinka	60
Lavender's blue (duet)	47
Little bird	29
Little playmates	7
London Bridge (duet)	54
London's burning (round)	52
Long, long ago (duet)	38
(Meet the) Flintstones	41
Merrily we roll along	19
Miss Mary Mac	25
Mobile phone	8
Morningtown ride	43
Muck! (round)	62
Nocturne	88
Ode to joy (duet)	39
Off to France in the morning	36
Old MacDonald	32
One finger dance (duet)	11
On top of Old Smokey (duet)	51
Part of your world (duet)	74
Pease pudding hot	20
Pizz A pizza!	2
Pizz on D	1
Pop! goes the weasel	67
Puff the magic dragon (duet)	64
Racing driver (round)	37
Ragamuffin's rag	84
Road monsters	22
Roses from the South	46
Row, row, row your boat (round)	66
Secret agents (duet)	28
Shalom (round)	72
Short'nin' bread (duet)	75
Skye boat song (duet)	57
Spinning wheel	13
Stand by me	56
Summer is icumen in (round)	73
Summer shine (duet)	30
Supercalifragilisticexpialidocious	5
Tea for two	55
The Addams family (duet)	81
The hippopotamus song	53
The mocking bird	82
The old bazaar in Cairo	61
The shepherdess (round)	69
The song that never stops (duet)	26
The way you look tonight	40
Troika	44
Turn the glasses over (round)	35
Twinkle, twinkle little bow	24
Waltz	63
We all stand together (duet)	49
Welsh lullaby (duet)	16
We're off to see the Wizard	70
What shall we do with the drunken sailor? (duet)	76
When the saints go marching in	4
Whistle while you work (duet)	27
Who will buy?	85
Windmill song (duet)	17
Winter wonderland	77

GLOSSARY

⊓	down-bow
V	up-bow
↻	lift bow in circular motion
+	left-hand pizzicato
D.C. al Fine	repeat from the beginning (Da Capo) up to Fine (the end)
D.S. al Fine	repeat from 𝄋 (the sign) up to Fine (the end)
s.b.	slow bow
f.b.	fast bow
⊓V⊓	zig-zag bowing pattern
V⊓V	zig-zag bowing pattern
	crescendo – get gradually louder
	diminuendo – get gradually quieter
⌒	pause
arco	with bow
ostinato	a repeated musical phrase
pizzicato (pizz.)	plucked
rallentando (rall.)	get gradually slower
staccato	short and detached
tenuto	with a light accent, lasting full length

p		(piano) quiet
f		(forte) loud
mp		(mezzo piano) moderately quiet
mf		(mezzo forte) moderately loud
allegro	–	fast and lively
andante	–	at a leisurely pace
cantabile	–	in a singing style
con fuoco	–	with fire
con spirito	–	with spirit
dolce	–	sweetly
espressivo	–	expressively
legato	–	smoothly
leggiero	–	lightly
maestoso	–	majestically
misterioso	–	mysteriously
moderato	–	at a moderate speed
tempo di valse	–	like a waltz